GRIMSHAW

Blue

WITHDRAWN

01 WATER, ENERGY AND WASTE

Contents

An Introduction to Blue by Andrew Whalley

01   ANDREW WHALLEY, SENIOR
     PARTNER OF GRIMSHAW NEW
     YORK, PICTURED IN FRONT OF
     THE EDEN PROJECT,
     CORNWALL, UK

Rigorous investigation, careful thought and the relentless testing of ideas has always been at the core of our work at Grimshaw. As the world's population grows in numbers and in wealth, we are accelerating the consumption of limited resources. Humanity now faces its most serious challenge to ensuring its continued and prosperous existence. Setting a new sustainable course for growth and development will take imagination, creativity, ingenuity, and, most importantly, the sharing of ideas in order to rapidly evolve a new relationship with our planet and conserve its precious resources.

Grimshaw's more investigative work often remains in the studio or lies concealed within the final constructed project. In response to issues of increasing global concern, we would like to share this investigation and thinking with our fellow colleagues; architects, designers, engineers and clients. We hope this process will enrich the quest for innovative solutions.

This approach was at the heart of our decision to restructure the company, now lead by a group of thirteen equal partners. This ensures that we are driven by our core beliefs and by our quest to find the optimum design solutions for our clients, rather than fiscal returns for shareholders. It is this shared passion that defines the Grimshaw Partnership.

Our first edition focuses on the issues surrounding Water, Energy and Waste. The introductory essay by Sir Nicholas Grimshaw describes the evolution of our own culture using six key projects, ranging from his early industrial work and influences to large scale projects of global recognition: The Eden Project, The British Pavilion for Expo, and the International Terminal Waterloo. We explore themes from city infrastructure to closed loop systems; within the context of food we range from very theoretical ideas on urban farming to Via Verde, an affordable housing project in the Bronx with a series of roof terraces forming an urban market garden. Our collection of essays on water is equally diverse, we feature a solar powered desalination system inspired by a Namibian fog beetle and the Croton Water Filtration Plant, also in the Bronx and currently under construction to supply part of Manhattan's drinking water.

Included in Sir Nicholas Grimshaw's opening essay is a photograph taken with Buckminster Fuller, outside his first project, The Service Tower. Since his first lecture in the late 1920s, Fuller's

02

02 ASSOCIATE DIRECTOR
    BILL HORGAN
03 DESIGN REVIEW WITH
    PARTNER VINCENT CHANG,
    CENTRE

Blue

We would welcome your thoughts and comments on any of the essays, which can be sent by email to;
blue@grimshaw-architects.com.

Our next issue will explore *Systems and Structures*.

___

By printing on paper made of 100 percent post consumer fiber this document prevented:

- 112 trees from being harvested

- 35 million BTUs of energy from being consumed, or the equivalent energy to power an American home for 140 days

- 51,133 gallons of water from entering the waste stream

- 10,616 lbs. of CO_2 and greenhouse gas equivalents being produced or the emmisions of one car driving for 351 days

- 3,104 lbs. of solid waste from entering the landfill

100 percent of the energy used to manufacture the paper and print this book came from Green-e certified Wind Energy. It was printed using soy based inks on paper that is certified by the Forestry Stewardship Council.

Designed by Neil Nisbet

© GRIMSHAW 2009

ISBN: 978-0-9825875-0-8

work has been unquestionably thought provoking and inspiring. Almost a century later his teachings and philosophies have never been more prophetic.

In his own words:

"All of humanity now has the option to 'make it' successfully and sustainably, by virtue of our having minds, discovering principles and being able to employ these principles to do more with less."

Buckminster Fuller

AN EVOLUTION OF IDEAS

Sir Nicholas Grimshaw CBE PRA
Chairman

I have always been driven by investigation, innovation and invention. These were traits that were strongly encouraged during my education at the Architectural Association in the sixties. It remains to this day one of the driving forces of our practice.

It is a piece of DNA that all of the Grimshaw Partners share in our exploration of architecture and the built environment. I have tried to encourage the spirit of enquiry in everything we do; from the proposal of a concept design to the development of a building detail. This issue of Blue is devoted to food and waste – both themes with an imperative in today's world, themes which should be considered as drivers for architecture. Both themes call for innovation and invention in the design of buildings.

As a background to the work and projects that are explored in this first issue of Blue I would like to pick out six Grimshaw projects which I think particularly express the pioneering spirit of our firm.

My first project started on July 1st 1965 – the day I left the Architectural Association. I had a relative who was involved in bringing students to London from Africa and finding them accommodation. His organisation had bought 6 vast houses, built in 1865, which had been neglected since the Second World War. The aim was to turn them into a hostel for 200 students but they had no plumbing or heating – or indeed any services at all.

01

WE MUST THINK ABOUT HOW WE CAN TAKE OUR EXISTING BUILDINGS AND RETROFIT THEM TO BUILD GREENER CITIES.

02

03

01 NICHOLAS GRIMSHAW
    EXPLAINS HIS CONCEPT FOR
    THE SERVICE TOWER TO
    RICHARD BUCKMINSTER
    FULLER, 1968

02 APARTMENTS, 125 PARK RD,
    LONDON UK, 1968
03 HERMAN MILLER ASSEMBLY
    PLANT, BATH UK, 1976

I devised a tower of bathrooms accessed by a spiral ramp which could be entered from any floor. Thus any student had full access to all 30 bathrooms. Mathematicians amongst you will know that this theoretically provides the maximum availability to everybody – all students needed to do was to keep walking round until they found a bathroom which was free.

This innovative layout was complemented by equally innovative methods of construction. The bathrooms were made in glass–reinforced plastic by a boat builder and craned into position using the structural core itself as the mast of the crane.

Thus began my fascination with using technology and new materials to create what I consider to be beautiful buildings. This adaptive re-use of existing buildings, utilising technology to give them a new lease of life and improving their environmental performance, is probably even more relevant forty years on. Our intervention allowed a very old building to have an entirely new function without destroying the integrity of the original. The helical ramp made stairs and lifts unnecessary. The structural core also acted as a new vertical riser for all the services and the end result brought six derelict houses back to life. I believe there is a very valuable lesson to be learned here. We must think about how we can take our existing buildings and retrofit them to build greener cities.

My second building was a block of 40 flats beside Regents Park in London. This was a co-operative housing project and the aim was to create the maximum amount of space for the lowest possible price. It was the first use of a central core in a residential building in London. We used a very simple concrete frame and clad it with ribbed aluminium and windows made by the same company that mass-produced windows for London buses. We built for the same price as public housing, but the spaces were genuinely flexible 'loft' spaces. They had concrete walls, floors and ceilings and total adaptability as to layout. This is now a building listed by English Heritage as a pioneering example of low-cost housing.

We continued developing this exploration and innovation in the field of industrial architecture. An early example is the 1977 factory for Herman Miller, the furniture manufacturer, outside the City of Bath in the UK.

Herman Miller wanted a factory with the potential for change because it did not know what lines it would be bringing out over the next twenty or thirty years. Our solution was an early use of fibreglass panelling to facilitate a very flexible skin.

Along with this adaptive cladding system on the outside was a very flexible servicing strategy inside. The combination of these two aspects allowed the building to behave like an organism that can adapt to suit the different demands placed on it.

Over the last twenty years the building has been completely rearranged five times. In the most recent change, the users moved the canteen to an area that was formerly used for manufacturing and so had an opaque skin; by moving glazed panels to this area, people could look out onto the river. This is an architecture that not only performs, but also improves the quality of life for its occupants.

The Eurostar International Terminal that we designed at London's Waterloo Station was our first major transport project. It is a very good example of our pursuit of a design concept through the resolution of key details. At that time the use of computers for CAD was limited to expensive main frame systems which meant (for the few offices which could afford them) that they were very limited in number and operated by specialists. We pioneered the use of a network of personal computers, with one for every architect on the team. This was seen as a very radical approach in 1988 – particularly as we were working on such a large, complex project. Now of course it's the norm.

01

01 **WATERLOO INTERNATIONAL RAIL TERMINAL, LONDON, 1993**
02 **PLAN VIEWS OF PLATFORM LEVEL AND ROOF**

Our approach was to produce a system of components to resolve a complex geometric envelope. The brief called for a very large roof, sheltering a terminal that is more like an airport than a railway station. It was designed to handle 15 million passengers, the size of Stansted Airport at the time – but right in the centre of London. The railway engineers gave us a complex footprint to accommodate trains coming into the station. Our brief for the roof, which was only 10% of the capital cost of the whole project, was to create some way of enclosing all that space, snaking its way to the terminus.

Again, a lot of time was spent in looking at manufacturing as we developed our ideas. We made many models as a way of visualising and understanding the space and structure and created a highly efficient asymmetrical form to suit the track layout. This allowed us to have the best of both worlds. We could follow the lead of the great Victorian railway sheds, where the structure is expressed internally, recreating the great halls of the nineteenth century. At the same time we could create an unprecedented public façade. The three-pin-arch form places the pin to one side,

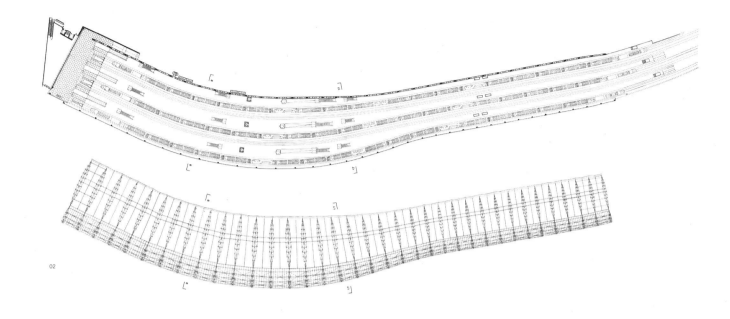

02

WE USED THE STRUCTURE TO ARTICULATE AND GIVE LIFE TO THE BUILDING AND ITS PUBLIC FACE, SOMETHING THE VICTORIAN STATION NEVER DID

responding to the asymmetrical nature of the platform layout. The pin forms the point of contraflecture, which effectively means that the compression and tensile elements are reversed. We used this as a device to invert the relationship of interior to exterior structure. We used the structure to articulate and give life to the building and its public face, something the Victorian station never did. We used the material only where it was needed structurally and, along-side the use of telescoping and tapering tubes, this produced a very dynamic skeleton-like form. We designed opaque cladding facing the station

and a glass elevation to the city, so that you can see the trains coming in and out.

The problem was, of course, how to create a glass envelope that can move and snake around the irregularly shaped site when the manufacturer insists that everything is standardised. So what we did – and this goes back to the DNA concept – was to design individual elements that would create the whole. The key element is a joint that was fabricated using the same technique as hip replacement joints – loss wax casting. The lattice has lots of rectilinear sheets of glass similar to a Victorian greenhouse.

The joint permits us to deal with different geometries by letting each sheet slide over the next – it is very much like the scales on a snake's skin. We spent a lot of time designing a single component, a joint element, which could pick up the skin anywhere in space. In this way we fulfilled our design concept and satisfied the manufacturer.

We certainly could not have designed it without computers, which we used to describe and explore the complex forms in three dimensions. Although it is all made out of rectilinear pieces of glass and tubular elements, it creates a very organic, fluid architecture.

01

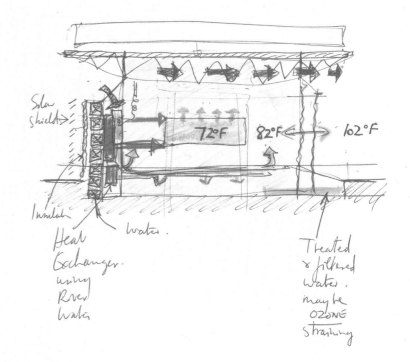

02

THE KEY CONCEPT WAS TO USE THE SUN TO COOL THE BUILDING

01 **BRITISH PAVILION, EXPO 1992, SEVILLE, SPAIN**
02 **EARLY SKETCH SHOWING TEMPERATURE CONCEPT**
03 **EDEN PROJECT, CORNWALL, UK, 2001**

I would now like to turn to sustainability and the search for an architectural form that is shaped as a response to its climatic setting. This interest for us started in earnest in the late eighties when we won a competition to design the British Pavilion for the World Expo 92 in Seville. We wanted to create a building suited to a very hot climate, one which responded to the environment it was placed in. The design of the building had to demonstrate what could be done with an ingenious approach to energy use by avoiding energy consuming mechanical plant. To achieve this we created an enclosure that tempered and controlled the environment within a number of highly conditioned pavilions. This also allowed for flexibility of use as the exhibition content was still to be established.

The key concept was to use the sun to cool the building. The roof was covered with photovoltaic cells. These were combined with fabric sails and used to shield the enclosure from the heat. The energy generated pumped water up and poured it over the glass, allowing light in but keeping the building cool. If you have a reasonable thickness of water, it will absorb almost all the infrared (heat) components of light, but will allow the rest of the spectrum into the building.

We further manipulated this idea of functional performance to give the space exceptional qualities that warmed or cooled the senses. We worked with sculptor William Pye who took the idea to develop the project's sculptural elements. He turned the water into droplets, which could be heard falling down as you walked through the space, so one could actually hear, see and understand what was cooling the building.

With my final project I would like to explore the whole field of biomimicry. This is the idea of developing high performance solutions that use nature as an inspiration to search for an optimum solution.

In Cornwall, southwest England, we have developed a project that explores the

03

minimisation of resource. The result, called the Eden Project, explores the planet from a botanical standpoint. Putting it in simple terms, its message is thus: without plants there would be no life on earth, no air, no food, no fossil fuels; they are the link between mankind and the planet's resources; they give the planet life. One of the enclosures had to be big enough to allow a rainforest to grow to its full maturity, which meant creating something about 50 metres high by 100 metres wide in cross section.

The site was a worked-out quarry, and our thinking was that half the architecture was there in the topography – an incredible landscape. What we had to do was capture elements of that landscape to create the enclosures. We wanted the architecture to have fluidity and a synergy to the topography that it nestled in.

Our goal was to build the lightest, most economical and environmentally benign structure possible.

Nature has many lessons to teach us with regard to structure; most obviously those concerning the minimum use of energy and the careful use of resources. What often appears to be fragile in nature is actually robust and has an inherent ability to adapt. A pollen seed demonstrates the exact geometry of Eden. The hexagonal pattern appears frequently in nature as the model for efficiency in absorbing and transferring stress.

The structure best suited to the geometry was made up of pentagons and hexagons. To minimise the size of the structural sections we used ETFE foil inflated pillows to glaze the forms. As we cut through the model, we get a changing fluid form – the topography of the ground changes and the enclosure changes. We simply captured air within the structure and the pneumatic skin.

Most importantly, we wanted the enclosure to be as light as possible for environmental reasons. We wanted it to be made out of small elements and from lightweight material, so it would require minimal transport to get the system down to what is the most remote part of England, poorly served by both the road and rail networks. The system is also light in its performance terms: the whole weight of the roof, including the steel and the foil, is no heavier than the mass of the air it encloses and the foil system uses 1% of the material volume of an equivalent glass solution. Ultimately, those are just facts and statistics, but for me, the functionality of the Eden Biomes give them great beauty.

To me these six projects are milestones in my own and Grimshaw's approach to innovation. But it is important to add that in every case the innovation has been for humanitarian reasons. For economy in the use of existing buildings; for flexibility to allow a long life for a building envelope; for repetition to allow components to be re-used and for harvesting energy to make buildings that sustain themselves.

I strongly believe that with the climate challenges we now face all buildings will have to be sustainable and energy-efficient by default. The challenge for architects is to make this manifest in their work, so that people again feel that architecture is about substance rather than style. ⓑ

Given the growing dema
services and other incr
ecosystems, the develo
technologies designed to
of resource use or redu
such as climate change
are essential.

Millennium Ecosystem Assessment, 2005
Ecosystems and Human Wellbeing – Synthesis

ds for ecosystem

sed pressures on

nent and diffusion of

ncrease the efficiency

the impacts of drivers

nd nutrient loading

CELEBRATING INFRASTRUCTURE

Jolyon Brewis
Partner

01

Hidden away, remote from the places we live and work, is the infrastructure that supports our lives.

Transportation systems, including roads, railways, bridges and underground stations, are visible within our cities, but other essential infrastructure is generally pushed out of our urban areas. It is relegated to distant locations, resulting in huge inefficiencies as power, food, water and waste all have to be transported miles to or from civilisation.

It was not always like this. 100 years ago, there were examples of energy, water and waste infrastructure in the hearts of our cities, built to celebrate the new technologies they housed. The advances in infrastructure and technology during this period improved lives by providing energy, delivering fresh water and improving sanitation and health. This was architecture that guaranteed a better future for the populace, and, as such was given prominence.

Examples of these buildings still exist today. In London, Battersea Power Station is now derelict but was originally called 'the Temple of Power'; Abbey Mills Pumping Station, designed in a cruciform shape and known locally as the 'Cathedral of

Sewage', is a stunning Byzantine-influenced structure and still in use today, albeit as an electrical back-up store for its contemporary replacement. Other examples can be found throughout the world.

Subsequently, the revolutions these buildings heralded became commonplace, and over time, infrastructure was no longer celebrated but taken for granted or,

even worse, rejected. Indeed, the polluting effects of infrastructure, particularly coal-fired power stations, became undesirable within urban areas. When coupled with the higher land values within cities, this led to a move towards locating infrastructure well away from conurbations.

We now use the term 'utilities' to describe the systems of power, water and sewerage

100 YEARS AGO, THERE WERE EXAMPLES OF ENERGY, WATER AND WASTE INFRASTRUCTURE IN THE HEARTS OF OUR CITIES, BUILT TO CELEBRATE THE NEW TECHNOLOGIES THEY HOUSED

that allow our society to operate, and the physical infrastructure to provide it has, in recent times, been utilitarian at best. As these facilities are out of sight, they are out of mind, runs the theory – so why expend more effort on them than is strictly necessary?

This need not be the case. Society is becoming increasingly aware of limited resources, wastefulness, and the impact of individual actions upon the environment. As a result, the construction of new infrastructure will be subject to increased scrutiny. New and innovative technologies for all forms of infrastructure are constantly emerging and we are increasingly finding ways to be cleaner and greener. These ingenious and forward-thinking solutions will come to be demanded by society over more outmoded technologies.

Furthermore, much of the infrastructure constructed in the last century needs to be replaced, either due to old age or obsolescence. In many cases, it is impossible to replace on a 'like-for-like' basis due to changes in demand or scarcity of supply. This further encourages the development and implementation of different forms of power generation, water supply and waste recovery, creating opportunities for a new design approach that helps to assimilate infrastructure more effectively into its context.

This new approach will partly rely on the installation of decentralised systems, more closely integrated with the communities they serve. Decentralisation will remove the inherent inefficiencies in older systems, where large-scale infrastructure was delivered via extensive distribution networks. Under this

system, developed in the last century and still in use today, a faulty power cable or water leak can cause a serious problem in the provision and delivery of utilities.

A decentralised system would rely far less on a distribution network, thus greatly reducing the opportunity for inefficiency. For this to happen, we will need to take a leaf from our predecessors' book by designing our infrastructure in such a way that we are proud to live alongside it.

The role of architecture in this next step will be vital to the success of decentralisation. It is only through design that the celebration of our infrastructure can be expressed, while a strong and appealing aesthetic will allow infrastructure to move back into our cities and resume its place within civilisation.

There is also an increasing understanding that to create truly sustainable urban development, all the systems involved need to be considered simultaneously. This will allow the potential for mutually beneficial relationships between supply and demand to be exploited for maximum benefit.

Architects have a vital part to play in this integration. They can demonstrate how the use of cleaner technologies can directly influence infrastructure's form; for instance, the development of technologies to neutralise gaseous emissions from power generation could mean the tall chimneys currently used to disperse them at a 'safe' height will, in time, become obsolete. Instead, new technologies, such as carbon capture and storage, or biological treatment using algae or plants, could lead to new expressions for these structures.

01

01 GOLF CLUBHOUSE AT CROTON
     WATER FILTRATION PLANT,
     NEW YORK, USA
02 THE TOMATO TOWER
03 ECO RAINFOREST

Increasingly, we will see waste, in the form of water, sewage, heat or refuse, as valuable raw material. It is this trend that lies at the centre of Grimshaw's theoretical 'Eco-Rainforest' greenhouse design.

The solution makes use of a household refuse landfill site to provide the fuel for the greenhouse's energy demands. A perimeter set series of large bio-digestion tanks process the organic element of the household waste. These tanks allow approximately 60% of landfill to be digested. The waste produces organic compost and, in doing so, generates

low-grade heat to warm the greenhouse. The principles behind this scheme could be used for productive greenhouses, perhaps supplying out-of-season or exotic fruit and vegetables with a vast reduction in food miles.

Another scheme, the Tomato Tower, takes advantage of the surplus heat within an underground railway station, and improves the environment within the station by drawing the heat away from the concourse. As the surplus heat is drawn up through the structure it warms the transparent tower enclosure; tomatoes

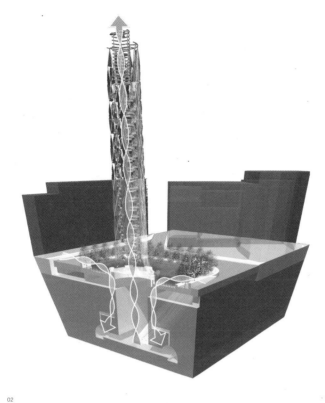

02

are grown hydroponically in trays that continually move up and down within the tower, ensuring even light levels to each plant. The tower provides a useful function in helping to cool the underground station, and acts as a landmark symbolising the transformation of unwanted heat into a productive crop.

The form of infrastructure can also be demonstrably influenced by its function, to create designs which are acceptable within city limits. This approach is central to our new Croton Water Filtration Plant, located in a Bronx park in New York City.

The design creatively integrates landscape and infrastructure, creating amenities for recreation and education. Water acts as the generating principle for the whole design, informing the site planning and the building design strategies. Alongside the water filtration facilities, the site will also contain a 9-hole public golf course, complete with clubhouse and driving range, plus an open civic space. All the new structures are built from locally sourced materials and fully integrated into the surrounding landscape.

Just as architecture played a role in celebrating the technologies that improved our lives a century ago, so it has a role again now. Excellent design will be essential if we seek to reintegrate and celebrate infrastructure within our communities, with all of the efficiencies and benefits that this could bring. ⑧

03

The problems associated v
contaminants are in genera
sewage, for instance — are
proportion to population si:
and contaminants reflect t
An affluent society uses a
volume of waste-producing
domestic trash and home-

h wastes and
growing. Some wastes—
roduced in nearly direct
. Other types of wastes
affluence of society.
generates a larger
materials such as
se chemicals.

Millennium Ecosystem Assessment, 2005
Ecosystems and Human Wellbeing – Synthesis

CLOSED LOOP SYSTEMS

Keith Brewis
Partner

Previously unquestioned habits associated with urban living, in particular its wastefulness and disconnection from nature, are starting to be understood as the greatest human threat and source of abuse of the earth's finite resources and its previously balanced eco-systems.

It is generally acknowledged that the demands placed by our cities lead to consumption of about 50% of all the resources we harvest or mine, and account for 75% of all our energy demands.

Most of the resources provided and manufactured for urban consumers have a high environmental cost and a short "shelf-life", with contaminated materials quickly discarded into land-fill. Most of our energy still comes from irreplaceable fossil fuels and this, together with the demands of our manufacturing industries and transport habits, produces the majority of emissions responsible for global warming and local climate change.

For the first time in history, cities now accommodate the majority of the human population, and whilst they seem to be an efficient use of land space – between 1% and 2% globally – their wasteful habits are no longer sustainable and are under intensive international scrutiny.

It seems clear that every resident needs to prepare to adjust their habits and to use and purchase "less stuff". Whilst this is obvious, it is also a threat to the basis

01 **PLASTIC BOTTLES AT A RECYCLING PLANT**
02 **BURNING OF FOSSIL FUELS**
03 **ENERGY MODEL FOR A SUSTAINABLE CITY**

of capitalism and to the demands of the previously unchallenged ideals of *growth of wealth*.

"Consuming less may be the single biggest thing you can do to save carbon emissions, and yet no one dares to mention it. Because if we did, it would threaten economic growth, the very thing that is causing the problem in the first place."

New Scientist, 15 October 2008
What politicians dare not say
by Tim Jackson

Perhaps though the greatest habitual change needs to emerge not from how little we purchase or use but instead by contemplating what we throw away, and by contemplating ways of not wasting waste.

Our speculative proposal for the Royal National Agricultural Society (RNA) site in Brisbane seeks to offer the city a demonstration project which also links to the core agricultural businesses of the Society members. It aims to subscribe to the values of the triple bottom line, where the environmental, economic and social issues are all considered together.

The RNA site is in the city-centre, within 2km of the Central Business District (CBD) and is surrounded by land designated for imminent, intensive

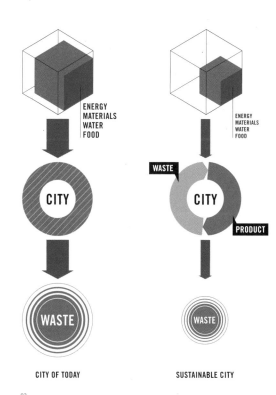

ENERGY
MATERIALS
WATER
FOOD

CITY

WASTE

CITY OF TODAY

ENERGY
MATERIALS
WATER
FOOD

WASTE

CITY

PRODUCT

WASTE

SUSTAINABLE CITY

03

THE GREATEST HABITUAL CHANGE NEEDS TO EMERGE NOT FROM HOW LITTLE WE PURCHASE OR USE, BUT INSTEAD FROM CONTEMPLATING WAYS OF NOT WASTING WASTE

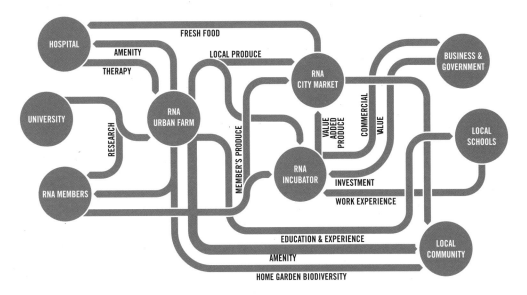

01

mixed-use developments to cater for population growth and the introduction of de-centralised Transit Oriented Developments (TODs).

We notice and suggest that there is a real opportunity to embrace agriculture and the science that supports it as a working urban insert. Not only might the community become a working model, it can also help to promote the environmental and social consciousness of the RNA Society and the city through tourism, education, and commerce, in a way not dissimilar to the Eden Project.

It is proposed that future land-use diagrams, including an intensive mix of uses, emerge not only from social analysis, but from contemplating what industry or person would use another's waste and coupling these locally to one another. As a demonstration project the new community is strategically planned to encourage businesses to congregate and tap into Closed Loop Systems to stimulate their own economies and the further growth of these systems. In effect the local community becomes tuned to use up everything.

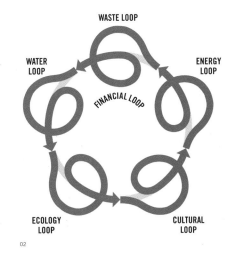

02

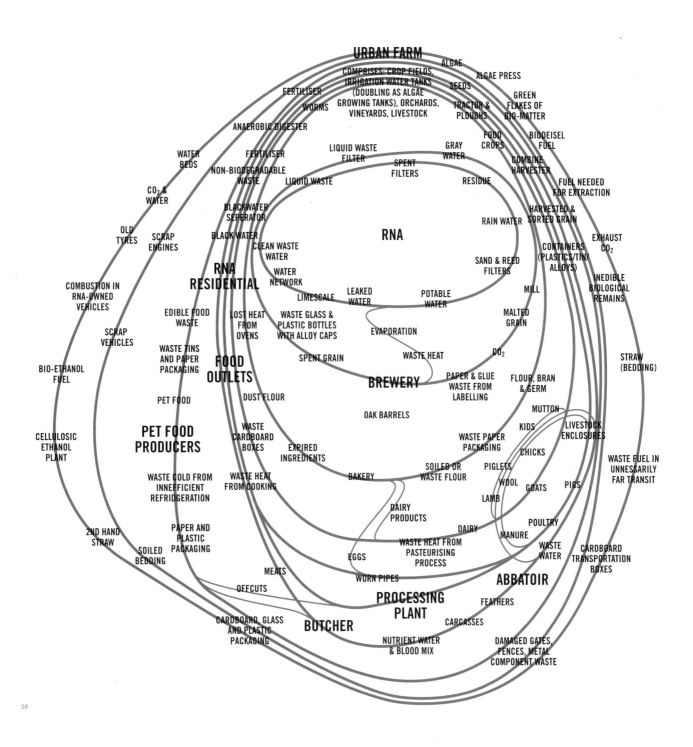

URBAN FARM

COMPRISES: CROP FIELDS, IRRIGATION WATER TANKS (DOUBLING AS ALGAE GROWING TANKS), ORCHARDS, VINEYARDS, LIVESTOCK

ALGAE
ALGAE PRESS
SEEDS
GREEN FLAKES OF BIO-MATTER
TRACTOR & PLOUGHS
FOOD CROPS
BIODEISEL FUEL
COMBINE HARVESTER
FUEL NEEDED FOR EXTRACTION
HARVESTED & SORTED GRAIN
EXHAUST CO₂
CONTAINERS (PLASTICS/TIN/ALLOYS)
INEDIBLE BIOLOGICAL REMAINS

FERTILISER
WORMS
ANAEROBIC DIGESTER
LIQUID WASTE FILTER
SPENT FILTERS
GRAY WATER
RESIDUE
RAIN WATER
SAND & REED FILTERS

WATER BEDS
FERTILISER
NON-BIODEGRADABLE WASTE
LIQUID WASTE
CO₂ & WATER
BLACKWATER SEPERATOR
BLACK WATER
CLEAN WASTE WATER
WATER NETWORK
RNA

RNA RESIDENTIAL

OLD TYRES
SCRAP ENGINES
LIMESCALE
LEAKED WATER
POTABLE WATER
MILL
MALTED GRAIN
STRAW (BEDDING)

COMBUSTION IN RNA-OWNED VEHICLES
EDIBLE FOOD WASTE
LOST HEAT FROM OVENS
WASTE GLASS & PLASTIC BOTTLES WITH ALLOY CAPS
EVAPORATION
CO₂

SCRAP VEHICLES
WASTE TINS AND PAPER PACKAGING
FOOD OUTLETS
SPENT GRAIN
WASTE HEAT
BREWERY
PAPER & GLUE WASTE FROM LABELLING
FLOUR, BRAN & GERM

BIO-ETHANOL FUEL
PET FOOD
DUST FLOUR
OAK BARRELS
WASTE PAPER PACKAGING
MUTTON
KIDS
LIVESTOCK ENCLOSURES

PET FOOD PRODUCERS
WASTE CARDBOARD BOXES
EXPIRED INGREDIENTS
SOILED OR WASTE FLOUR
CHICKS
PIGLETS

CELLULOSIC ETHANOL PLANT
WASTE COLD FROM INNEFFICIENT REFRIDGERATION
WASTE HEAT FROM COOKING
BAKERY
WOOL
GOATS
PIGS
WASTE FUEL IN UNNESSARILY FAR TRANSIT

LAMB
PAPER AND PLASTIC PACKAGING
DAIRY PRODUCTS
DAIRY
POULTRY
MANURE
WASTE WATER

2ND HAND STRAW
SOILED BEDDING
EGGS
WASTE HEAT FROM PASTEURISING PROCESS
CARDBOARD TRANSPORTATION BOXES

MEATS
WORN PIPES
ABBATOIR

OFFCUTS
PROCESSING PLANT
FEATHERS

CARDBOARD, GLASS AND PLASTIC PACKAGING
BUTCHER
CARCASSES

NUTRIENT WATER & BLOOD MIX
DAMAGED GATES, FENCES, METAL COMPONENT WASTE

03

31

The emerging mix of uses should clearly help to drive other social and economic benefits.

In this model the output of buildings including CO_2, heat, contaminated water and black water are collected. The introduction of various filters (including aquaponics and open swales) and "at-source separators" (urine diversion toilets, for example) allows re-use of water for cooling, heating, recreation, drinking, irrigation and agriculture, and the introduction of bio-gas reactors allows re-use of black water solids to energy.

It seems that it is the coupling of local agriculture that may have the most profound effect. The inputs for growing – water, nutrients, heat and CO are available by the "bucket load" yet to date cities have simply discharged them without question. Although at the RNA site the land available for large scale food growth is not huge in area, agricultural space will be readily available. There is planned usage of building's surface area, through cropping terraces, and roof crop greenhouses with hydroponic growing, plus more conventional agriculture in green wedges or green belts around the city.

Incidentally at the RNA site Brisbane's major general hospital sits on the doorstep. Not only is the hospital a fantastic source of waste, water, heat and CO_2, the introduction of growing gardens

01

IT SEEMS THAT IT IS THE COUPLING OF LOCAL AGRICULTURE THAT MAY HAVE THE MOST PROFOUND EFFECT

Image courtesy of Goode Green

01 URBAN FARMING IN
    BROOKLYN, NEW YORK
02 GREENHOUSE UTILISING
    HYDROPONIC GROWTH
    METHODS

02

on its doorstep would provide a working community healing garden for its patients who are convalescing or struggling to motivate their healing process.

The introduction of an urban farm and agribusiness not only allows direct re-use of waste, via composting, but it also diminishes "food miles" and starts to address the surging world food crisis, particularly in new capitalist economies. This locally produced food can clearly link to local produce markets and local restaurants that become of their place, climate and season rather than multi-national corporate entities

The collective industry would help to stimulate the desired trend towards community functions – people of the community working for the community and would help to trend cities away from the psychological and serious health consequences of humanity's disconnect from nature as espoused by Richard Louv in his book, *Last Child in the Woods.* Ⓑ

Global demand for food crops is projected to grow by 70–8

5% between 2000 and 2050

Millennium Ecosystem Assessment, 2005
Ecosystems and Human Wellbeing – Synthesis

BLUE ISSUE 01
OCTOBER 2009

FROM FIELD TO FORK

Ben Heath
Associate

In collaboration with
Eric Osborne

The BT Tower is an eye-catching element of London's skyline, located in the central area of Fitzrovia. Its construction began in 1961 and the tower was officially opened in 1965, by Prime Minister Harold Wilson. Today, it is a major UK communications hub. The tower's main structure is 177m (581 ft), increasing to 189m (620ft) with the aerial. The structure was Grade II listed in 2003 and there are no plans to redevelop the site in any way, shape or form.

The following article is purely theoretical and its content is in no way a comment on the site's current design or use. It is speculation on the alternative possibilities offered by such an iconic building and site, informed by the current need for sustainable and self-sufficient buildings.

This hypothetical scenario proposed a replacement design for the BT tower and asked what an environmentally innovative tall building (not necessarily owned by BT) for that site might look like. How tall could it go? What would be its main use(s)? What would the key sustainability features be? Should there be public accessibility to its upper reaches? And how, in credit-crunch-affected times, could its energy innovations be affordable and pay dividends?

From Field to Fork is a proposal for a vertical farm that functions as part of a sustainable closed system food production centre. Rotating agricultural plates and a roof level grazing plateau would generate

WIND TURBINE: built up to the maximum permitted aeronautical height, this provides electrical demand for development. In addition, associated waterborne vibrations in tank aid oxygenation stimulate fish growth.

FISH TANK: the upper level beacon functions as London's urban lighthouse, water collection site and heat sink, and provides nutrient enriched water for irrigation of the agricultural decks below. These are heated using waste heat from greenhouse and biogas production.

GREENHOUSE: ETFE encapsulated decks provide protection against wind burn and provide out of season or non-regional production for exotic fruits, grape vines, french beans etc.

AGRICULTURAL DECKS: Plate cut-outs or a profile in conjunction with rotation is designed to provide crop specific optimisation of daily, direct sunlight allowance. A combination of hydroponics and traditional agricultural techniques would be used.

LIVESTOCK: Fed waste products from agricultural activity and waste produce is collected and fed into an onsite biogas generator for localised heating.

GRAZING PLATEAU: This is made up of livestock husbandry, a city farm and picnic areas

PROCESSING BLOCK: The existing structural frame houses an abattoir; a processing and packaging plant; veterinary services; ancillary accommodation; food outlets; restaurants and bars; and supporting commercial space.

GROUND FLOOR PLANE: Along with an anchor supermarket selling onsite farm produce, a significant percentage of the ground floor plan is given over to the public. This facilitates intuitive routes up to the new rooftop landscape and provides an associated urban space for curated or spontaneous happenings. These might include a food market, street parties, cow dancing, chicken racing and sheep rodeo.

01

02

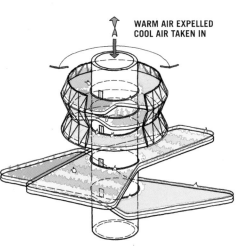

WARM AIR EXPELLED
COOL AIR TAKEN IN

04

01 BT TOWER, LONDON
02 CONCEPT DRAWING OF THE
    COMPLETE SCHEME
03 DRAWING OF ROTATING
    AGRICULTURAL PLATES
04 STREET LEVEL PERSPECTIVE
    DRAWING

over two hectares of arable land using biointensive farming techniques. These would then link to an on-site abattoir; a processing and packaging plant; restaurants; wholesalers; a street level anchor supermarket; and a new public space.

We took our cue from escalating food prices, ever increasing transport costs and the predicted loss of the global bread basket through a combination of climate change, soil erosion, salinisation and water logging, to design a project that is completely self sufficient in terms of food production. With over half of the world's population currently living in cities, and set to increase further, evidence suggests that in the future it will be compulsory for large urban centres to provide at least some of their agricultural requirements.

With an existing building the most sustainable option will nearly always involve reuse and reinvention. The fact that the BT Tower is a Grade II listed structure only adds weight to this strategy. As a consequence, we looked at retaining the existing podium structure, the structural tower core and the much loved high-level revolving restaurant. To our minds, these building elements retain the iconic nature of the existing tower and also encompass the massive structural concrete frame in which the vast majority of the building's embodied energy is contained.

In economically uncertain times it is the bold move that wins the day. The ideas contained within From Field to Fork aim to capture the public imagination, breathe new life into an urban area and kick start a localised economic boom. ⓑ

Innovative approache
needs are called for
beyond the belief tha
necessarily entails m
especially in societie
needs are already be

to meeting human
we are to move
greater well-being
re consumption,
where basic
ng met.

World Wilderness Foundation
Living Planet Report 2006

VIA VERDE

Robert Garneau
Senior Architect

01

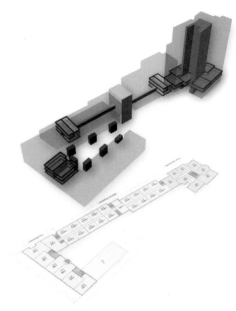

02

"Ultimately what we liked the most about this winning design, 'Via Verde', was that it took the definition of sustainability to another level; we thought this project was a great example of a different kind of sustainability, of a community sustainability that can be a real model for other work in affordable housing."

SHAUN DONOVAN
US Secretary of Housing and Urban Development (former Commissioner of NYC Department of Housing Preservation and Development)

01 **AREA MAP SHOWING CONSTRAINED SITE CONDITIONS**	03 **PERSPECTIVE RENDERING FROM THE STREET**
02 **DIAGRAM WITH MASSING AND UNIT TYPOLOGIES**	04 **PERSPECTIVE RENDERING FROM THE TOP ROOF**
	05 **LANDSCAPED ROOF PLAN**

In 2006 Grimshaw won the first juried design competition for affordable housing in the history of New York City. The competition was jointly launched by the New York City Department of Housing Preservation and Development, the American Institute of Architects, the New York State Energy Research and Development Authority and Enterprise Community Partners.

Grimshaw successfully responded to a brief calling for replicability, sustainability and 'healthy living' principles in the hope that this scheme will be a model for future developments in the city. Grimshaw is collaborating with Dattner Architects, and a pair of developers: Phipps Houses, the city's largest non-profit affordable housing developer and property manager; and Jonathan

03

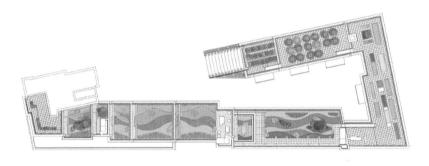

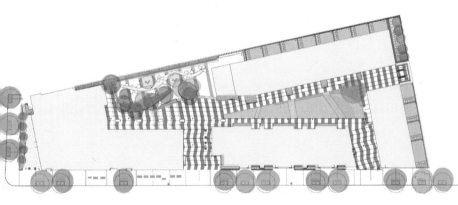

Rose Companies, a leading developer of sustainable, affordable housing.

The project takes as its reference point the dialogue between city and garden that has animated the history of urban design. Whereas Ebenezer Howard and Le Corbusier suggested macro responses through the radical transformation of entire cities and regions; we propose a more modest, grass-roots based solution. We believe that within one city block in the Bronx, we can demonstrate a range of urban living opportunities that can be equally transformative by modelling healthy, sustainable, urban living.

The site, a Brownfield left over from a former rail yard and gas station, had been derelict for more than 40 years. Over the years there were many attempts to develop the site but without any success, partially due to its soil contamination but mostly due to the awkward site dimensions. The 500ft (150m) long site is only 40ft (12m) on one end and 130ft (40m) wide at the other, with a 20ft (6m) deep defunct rail corridor along the long edge.

The proposed scheme is a mixed-use, mixed-income residential development in the middle of the South Bronx, a burgeoning urban neighbourhood. To support this revitalisation we are providing street level amenities to activate the street life: landscaped public plaza, food co-op store, community health clinic and live/work units. There are a total of 222 residential units, of which 71 units are for sale to middle-income households and the rest will be low and moderate-income rentals. The building consists of a 20-story tower, a mid-rise building with duplex apartments and walk-up town-houses. The massing is a direct response to the neighbouring 18-storey building on the north and a high school playing field on the south, but also about reducing self shading by tapering the building towards the south.

While our solution is fundamentally urban in terms of density and amenities, at its heart lies a dynamic garden that serves as the organising element and focal identity for the residents. The key concept is a series of roof terraces spiralling from the top down to a central courtyard, offering residents access to a series of communal landscape. Our gardens are multifunctional, creating opportunities for active gardening, fruit and vegetable cultivation, passive recreation and social gathering.

The vegetated landscape also has the added benefit of mitigating the strong regional heat island effect, as well as reducing peak storm water discharges that pollute the rivers due to the combined sewer system being overtaxed. However the most important attribute of the gardens is that it allows the members of the Via Verde community, through a variety of open space experiences, to benefit from a profound connection to the natural environment, while enjoying the benefits of urban living.

Some of the other environmental attributes of the project include the following: A 30% energy saving thanks to a mix of passive design techniques

01

02

01 **SECTION THROUGH ROOF PLANTERS**
02 **SECTION THROUGH VEGETATED ROOF**
03 **PERSPECTIVE RENDERING FROM THE ROOF GARDEN**

and a judicious use of cost-effective technologies. All the south faces of the cascading roofs have photovoltaic arrays providing 5% of the overall building electricity requirements. Rainwater is collected from all the roofs, stored in an underground cistern for reuse on-site. Each apartment has two facades allowing plenty of cross-ventilation and excellent daylight, interior finishes include low VOC finishes, as well as water and energy conserving fixtures. The building envelope is very well sealed and insulated, consisting of large prefabricated rainscreen panels with composite wood, cement and metal finishes. LEED Gold is anticipated with a special focus on innovation in promoting health and wellness by the use of active design measures.

The project offers 60,000sf (5600m²) of landscaping for the residents of Via Verde with a mix of hardscape for walking and playing as well as over 18,000sf (1700m²) of planted area. Roughly half of the vegetated areas are on the roofs and the other half is at grade. Landscaped areas are handicap accessible and most of the roof landscaping will not require irrigation, but where needed it will be drip irrigation fed by harvested rainwater.

The building is tallest to the north of the site and sets back from the street edge accordingly. A public plaza is provided here and serves as a forecourt to a planned health food co-op store. The plaza is sized to allow a small bi-weekly farmers market to take place, an opportunity for regional farmers and resident gardeners to interact

and provide fresh local food to the South Bronx community.

There is a single entrance into the housing complex that gives into a protected, private courtyard. The southern part of the courtyard serves as the front yard for walk up townhouses with exterior stairs. A central meadow with perimeter planters provides a serene environment for the residents.

Along the northern portion of the courtyard is a raised children play area: a sinuous 'dry-riverbed' landscape with large boulders, deciduous trees, and a colourful resilient safety surface. Along the property line a vegetated wall with built-in seating and table acts as a backdrop to this raised stage area.

To the south of the raised play area, an amphitheatre gently steps down from the green roofs merging into the ground plane. It acts as a seating area for viewing outdoor activities below; children playing and outdoor performances, or simply as a social gathering space. Both sides of the seated area are planted with wintercreeper evergreen vines and punctuated by pyramidal yews to maintain a green ribbon of vegetation.

The lowest green roof, located on top of the townhouses, is planted with evergreens. A mix of scots pine, concolor fir and Serbian spruce ensures greenery all year round visible from the main entrance into the complex.

The next level up on the roof is a beautiful orchard in wood planters. These are dwarf fruit bearing trees such as pears, apples and peaches, adding colour most of the year from the spring blossoms to the fall harvest.

On the largest roof we have one of the key features of the project, a place for the residents to grow food in their own individual plots. This garden will provide fresh, highly nutritious, locally grown food for families with very low incomes, this will be a cost effective means for them to eat the healthiest food.

Moving along the roof, straddling the street and the courtyard, there is a rooftop fitness centre with a large vegetated green roof. A covered deck and walkway offers a shaded place for outdoor exercising. A Japanese Black Pine tree is the focal point of this roof surrounded by a variety of sedums.

The next six levels of roofs are lush green and not accessible to the residents in order to promote biodiversity. There are a few trees but the area will consist mainly of drought tolerant plants such as allium, green sedum, red sedum, and flamegrass, with a band of tall switch grass along the western edge that is visible from the street below.

At the top of the building residents have access to a landscaped terrace adjacent to the community room. From here one has expansive views overlooking the Bronx and Manhattan, the green carpet of Via Verde unfurling at their feet in a gentle cascade of vegetation. ⊙

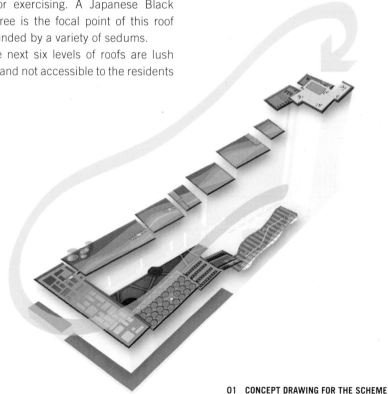

01

01 CONCEPT DRAWING FOR THE SCHEME

Physical and economic wat
or reduced access to water
facing society and are key f
development in many count
resource developments un
to water have not given ade
trade-offs with other servic

scarcity and limited

re major challenges

tors limiting economic

es. However, many water

rtaken to increase access

ate consideration to harmful

provided by wetlands.

Millennium Ecosystem Assessment, 2005
Ecosystems and Human Wellbeing – Synthesis

BLUE ISSUE 01
OCTOBER 2009

WATER SYSTEMS FOR URBAN IMPROVEMENT

David Burke
Associate

In collaboration with
Mark Laska, Great Eastern Ecology

Water is a vital resource which dramatically affects the well being of our planet. Water regulates the earth's temperature, it also regulates the temperature of the human body, carries nutrients and oxygen to cells, cushions joints, protects organs and tissues, and removes wastes. Industries as well as people need water. It takes, on average, 39,090 gallons of water to manufacture a new car and its four tires. Yet we are in a global water crisis where at any given time half of all hospital beds throughout the world are filled with those suffering from water related diseases. Now more than ever, is the time when our population needs to conserve water, whether by saving water at home or on a larger scale developing city infrastructure that responds to this crisis and uses sensible building practices to reduce its overall water footprint. On a civic scale, we will discuss a project that retains storm and ground water on site, polishes it naturally within constructed wetlands to reduce or completely eliminate discharge into the city sewer; ultimately conserving potable water for those citizens of New York who need it most.

When water moves along or through the earth, either via storm or ground water, there is the potential for it to collect sediments, and, in developed areas, a variety of chemicals such as fertilisers (phosphorous and nitrogen), trace heavy metals, oils

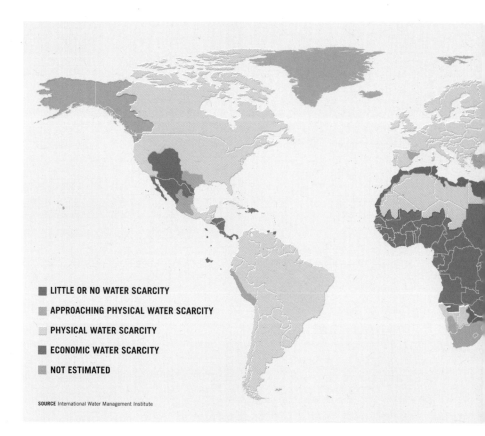

LITTLE OR NO WATER SCARCITY

APPROACHING PHYSICAL WATER SCARCITY

PHYSICAL WATER SCARCITY

ECONOMIC WATER SCARCITY

NOT ESTIMATED

SOURCE International Water Management Institute

01

02

NOW MORE THAN EVER OUR POPULATION
NEEDS TO CONSERVE WATER

from cars and machinery, and other contaminants or substances. If these materials reach natural water systems they can adversely affect the health and well-being of humans and wildlife.

Wetlands are natural systems that can *process* water, purifying it as it moves through the system. Natural wetlands filter water several ways: by binding contaminants in the sediments; by microbial activity which breaks down pollutants; and by plant uptake of nutrients. Of course, natural wetlands perform many other functions as well – they provide flood retention during storms, provide habitat to wildlife and fish, and are among the most productive ecosystems on the planet.

Over the past twenty years a large movement has grown in the US and Europe to build *treatment wetlands*. These are constructed wetlands that seek to mimic the benefits of natural ones. These wetlands can be built for a variety of reasons – they can be utilised to help process municipal wastewater, such as sewage; they can be used for treatment of industrial effluent; or they can be used to reduce sediments and pollutants that occur in large landscapes.

Treatment systems can range in size, from large tracts of wetlands built to improve water quality in the Everglades, to small, intensive *living machines* enclosed in a system of tanks and pipes. At least 5000 constructed treatment systems are in use in Europe and there are estimated to be over 1000 in the US.

Many constructed wetlands are designed and built to act as *secondary polishing systems*, handling water that has already passed through an engineered treatment system where the majority of water

01

01 ARCATA WASTE WATER
    MARSH PROJECT IN
    CALIFORNIA
02 AERIAL VIEW OF CROTON
    WATER TREATMENT PLANT

02

purification occurs. These engineered systems may be chemical (a substance may be added that binds to the contaminant and removes it from the system) or they might be mechanical (filters that remove the contaminant). Wetlands act as secondary polishing systems and remove the remaining contaminants or sediments from the water.

Constructed treatment wetlands can accept water either through surface flow (i.e. water that sheets across the surface of the wetland) or via subsurface flow (that moves under the vegetated layer). Water is treated differently in each of these systems – surface flow is dominated by plant processing while subsurface flow is treated more by the wetland sediments.

These systems are constructed by selecting a site and excavating to the appropriate depth, then backfilling with sediments, soils and grading so that water moves in the desired direction. Sediments are planted with wetland vegetation, and weirs or other structures are built to control water flow and volume. Wetlands are also lined with an impermeable fabric to prevent infiltration. Over the long term, the manager of the wetlands is responsible for monitoring and maintaining them in a natural state.

A designer's goal for treatment wetlands is to slow water flow, making the system large enough for the water to remain in contact with the wetland for as long as possible. This interaction time should be maximised, either with sediments, where contaminants can be bound up and retained by the soil, or with plants and their associated

01

microbes, in order to absorb and/or break-down pollutants. Treatment systems can be quite large – the Beaumont TX municipal wastewater treatment system is over 900 acres and attracts 350 species of birds; the San Antonio system is almost 600 acres in size; Arcata, California's wastewater marsh project is 150 acres; and the Sacramento California demonstration treatment wetlands are almost 22 acres in size.

As part of the recent sustainable design movement, smaller scale systems have been employed at countless sites. These smaller systems can be incorporated into site plans for commercial and/or residential development. They include vegetated bioswales that direct and process storm water or rain gardens which are depressed areas that collect water and process it using native vegetation. Rain gardens and bioswales can process water or act as conduits to direct water into other conveyance systems. These concepts were almost unheard of a decade ago – today they are employed by countless architects, landscape architects, planners, ecologists and site designers.

Grimshaw has designed a sophisticated storm and groundwater management system that demonstrates these principles at our Croton Water Treatment Plant project in the Bronx, New York City. Since 1847 the Croton Watershed was first tapped for New York City's public water supply, city residents have drunk water directly from the watersheds of upstate New York. NYC is still one of the few cities fortunate enough to have direct access to potable water filtered entirely by nature. However,

the Croton Watershed, located from 45 miles north of the city, has become increasingly developed in recent years. Increases in infrastructure, landfills, and runoff as well as naturally occurring organic changes in the water have endangered the quality of Croton water. Consequently, in November of 1998 a consent decree entered into by the United States District Court between the City of New York, New York State and the United States Federal Government agreed to site, design and construct a facility to filter water from the Croton Watershed.

The new Croton Water Treatment Plant is New York City's first water filtration facility. Located in Van Cortlandt Park in the Bronx, it will include emerging sustainable practices on both a civic

scale and a technical level. Grimshaw and a team of ecologists, landscape architects and civil engineers have designed a sophisticated hydrological and ecological approach to site planning and building design. Through the use of runnels, bioswales, and rain gardens, the project demonstrates best practice for storm water management as well as advanced storm and ground water reuse strategies to minimise the effect of storm water runoff and to eliminate discharge of water into the sewer.

The water treatment plant is currently being constructed below grade and will be covered by the restoration of Van Cortlandt Park above it. Grimshaw is designing the 34-acre landscape together with several integrated building

types. These buildings include the Water Treatment Plant entrance facilities, the Department of Parks and Recreation (DPR) Mosholu Golf Course driving range; club house and tee boxes. Coupled with this unique program, the site must be made secure to protect the facility below ground and to ensure the delivery of potable water to the citizens of New York City. The strategic positioning of landscape features such as site walls, runnels and constructed wetlands provide the secured perimeter road.

As is the case with the Croton Watershed,

the site at the Mosholu Golf Course will have a decrease in permeable surface with the introduction of the 9-acre water treatment plant. This increase in impervious surfaces will increase runoff into the city's combined sewer. Consequently, the design team has reviewed the site's natural drainage characteristics and found an opportunity to use the natural topography to redirect storm and ground water by gravity to strategic locations for treatment and storage rather than discharging the water into the city's combined sewer.

Both ground water and storm water

01   ENTRANCE PLAZA AT
      THE MOSHOLO GOLF COURSE
      CLUBHOUSE

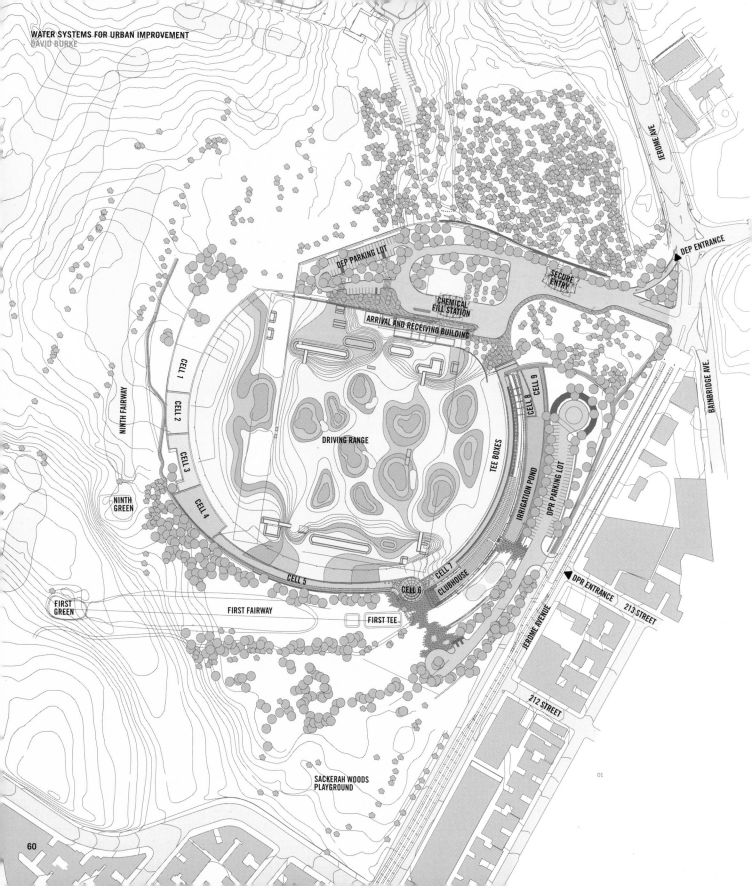

JEROME AVE.

DEP ENTRANCE

DEP PARKING LOT

SECURE ENTRY

CHEMICAL FILL STATION

ARRIVAL AND RECEIVING BUILDING

NINTH FAIRWAY

CELL 1

CELL 2

CELL 3

CELL 4

NINTH GREEN

DRIVING RANGE

CELL 8

CELL 9

TEE BOXES

IRRIGATION POND

DPR PARKING LOT

BAINBRIDGE AVE.

CELL 5

CELL 7

CELL 6

CLUBHOUSE

FIRST GREEN

FIRST FAIRWAY

FIRST TEE

DPR ENTRANCE

213 STREET

JEROME AVENUE

212 STREET

SACKERAH WOODS PLAYGROUND

01

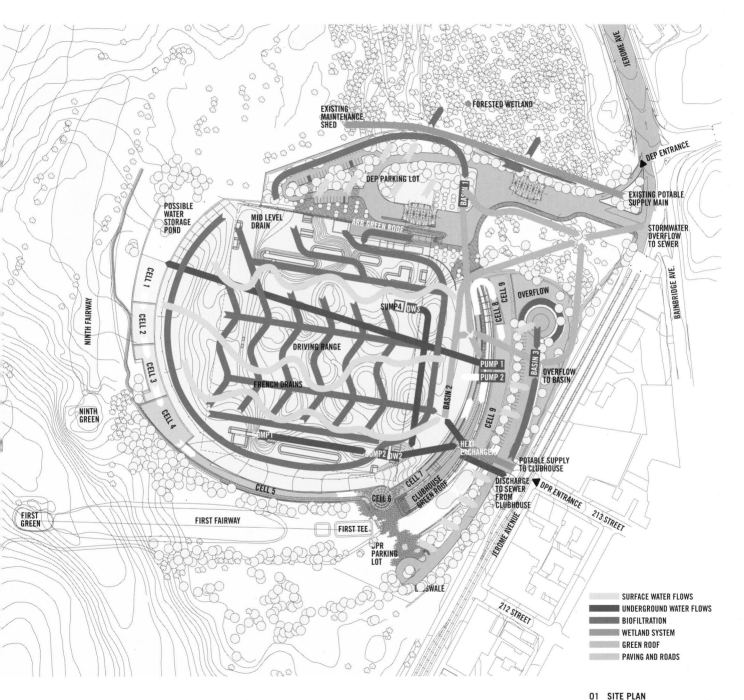

JEROME AVE

FORESTED WETLAND

EXISTING
MAINTENANCE
SHED

DEP PARKING LOT

DEP ENTRANCE

EXISTING POTABLE
SUPPLY MAIN

POSSIBLE
WATER
STORAGE
POND

MID LEVEL
DRAIN

ARB GREEN ROOF

BASIN 1

STORMWATER
OVERFLOW
TO SEWER

BAINBRIDGE AVE.

CELL 1

NINTH FAIRWAY

CELL 2

CELL 3

CELL 4

NINTH
GREEN

SUMP4 DW3

CELL 8 CELL 9

OVERFLOW

DRIVING RANGE

FRENCH DRAINS

BASIN 3

PUMP 1
PUMP 2

OVERFLOW
TO BASIN

SUMP1

SUMP2 DW2

BASIN 2

CELL 9

HEAT
EXCHANGERS

POTABLE SUPPLY
TO CLUBHOUSE

CELL 5

CELL 7

CLUBHOUSE
GREEN ROOF

CELL 6

DISCHARGE
TO SEWER
FROM
CLUBHOUSE

DPR ENTRANCE

213 STREET

FIRST
GREEN

FIRST FAIRWAY

FIRST TEE

DPR
PARKING
LOT

JEROME AVENUE

SWALE

212 STREET

SURFACE WATER FLOWS
UNDERGROUND WATER FLOWS
BIOFILTRATION
WETLAND SYSTEM
GREEN ROOF
PAVING AND ROADS

01 SITE PLAN
02 WATER FLOW PLAN DIAGRAM

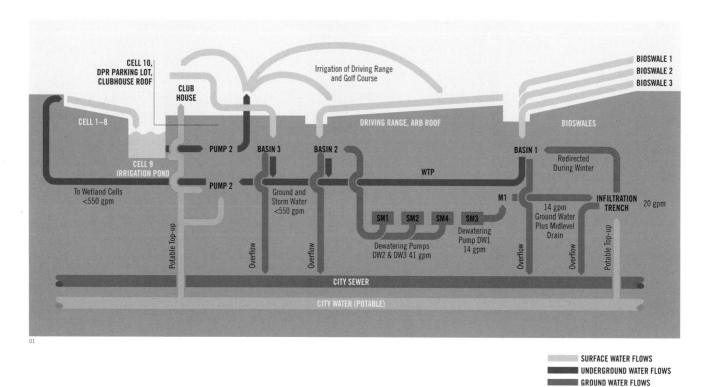

CELL 10,
DPR PARKING LOT,
CLUBHOUSE ROOF

CLUB
HOUSE

BIOSWALE 1
BIOSWALE 2
BIOSWALE 3

Irrigation of Driving Range
and Golf Course

CELL 1–8

DRIVING RANGE, ARB ROOF

BIOSWALES

PUMP 2

BASIN 3

BASIN 2

BASIN 1

Redirected
During Winter

CELL 9
IRRIGATION POND

PUMP 2

WTP

M1

INFILTRATION
TRENCH   20 gpm

To Wetland Cells
<550 gpm

Ground and
Storm Water
<550 gpm

14 gpm
Ground Water
Plus Midlevel
Drain

SM1   SM2   SM4   SM3

Dewatering
Pump DW1
14 gpm

Dewatering Pumps
DW2 & DW3 41 gpm

Potable Top-up

Overflow

Overflow

Overflow

Overflow

Potable Top-up

CITY SEWER

CITY WATER (POTABLE)

01

SURFACE WATER FLOWS
UNDERGROUND WATER FLOWS
GROUND WATER FLOWS
POTABLE WATER SUPPLY
SEWER OVERFLOW

make up vast quantities of water that would otherwise be discharged into the sewer. Our challenge is to collect, clean and store this water on site. Beginning below grade, round water seeps through the bedrock and is deposited at the base of the water treatment plant. From here it is collected and moved by dewatering pumps up to retention basins near the surface. An estimated 55 gallons per minute will be collected here.

Rain water will also be collected and retained in these underground basins. A nine acre green roof located on top of the

plant will see the largest water volumes.

Finally, a system of bioswales and runnels collect the remainder of site storm-water runoff from roadways and parking lots. The swales move water across a planted system designed to absorb water and process parking lot contaminants, such as suspended sediment, heavy metals, and petroleum products. At the end of the swales, remaining water drains into the storage basins to join collected ground and other site storm water.

Following its collection from the base

of the plant and surface areas, the storm and ground water is pumped to a high point on the site and discharged into an on-grade constructed wetland system. Consisting of 10 individual treatment cells, the water, led by gravity, flows naturally downhill without the use of pumps, pipes or valves. Consequently, these 'moats' also serve as natural security boundaries, which protect the plan and eliminate the need for unsightly fencing.

The 10 treatment cells encircle the entire 9-acre Water Treatment Plant. The first four cells are designed as a mixed surface

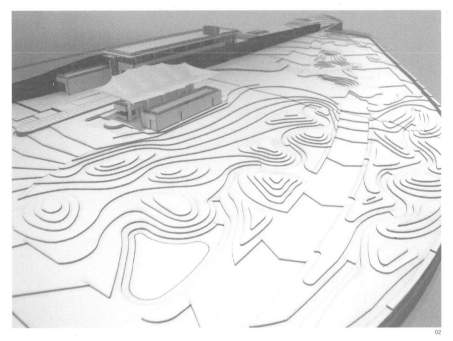

01   WATER FLOW SECTION
     DIAGRAM
02   MODEL OF THE SITE

and subsurface flow system, planted with emergent vegetation and exposed to high light conditions. Most of the polishing will occur in this area as suspended sediments drop out, plants uptake dissolved nutrients, and microbes break down petroleum-related materials.

Cells 5, 6 and 7 are narrow and increase water velocity. They have a rocky bottom with fewer plants. Agitation created by these conditions adds dissolved oxygen further polishing the water. Cell 6 has a 'mist' system in place to encourage the growth of ferns and mosses. It is designed as a waterfall feature.

The water completes its journey around the site finding its way into cell 9, the irrigation pond. Here the aerated and polished water is collected and stored and will be used for irrigation and building maintenance purposes. The driving range and 9 hole golf course will use up to 280,000 gallons per month during peak summer season, to minimise, or even eliminate, the use of potable water for golf course irrigation. The majority of this water will come from the storm and ground water collection system. The collected storm and ground water will also be used

for building maintenance such as vehicle and building washing.

Furthermore, in recent years flash flooding has been damaging and costly to the city. New York has been affected more often by flooding than by drought as is the case in other parts of the world.

The New York City 'combined sewer system' shares both storm water and sewage. Flash flooding increases water volume to the sewer system beyond its capacity causing sewage treatment plants to divert this water into local streams and rivers during extreme storm events, ultimately polluting our natural environment. Flooding causes delays in traffic and public transportation and causes damage to homes and buildings that require money and effort to repair.

Retaining our water on site through the use of constructed bioswales, wetlands and retention systems and preventing discharge into the sewer system supports both our environment and our local infrastructure, while reusing this water for non-potable uses such as irrigation and building uses limits the use of potable water and increases conservation.

The Above Ground Buildings and Landscape at the Croton Water Treatment Plant will showcase these strategies on a scale not commonly seen, and it is helping to make best practices of storm water management a standard practice among future development. ⊖

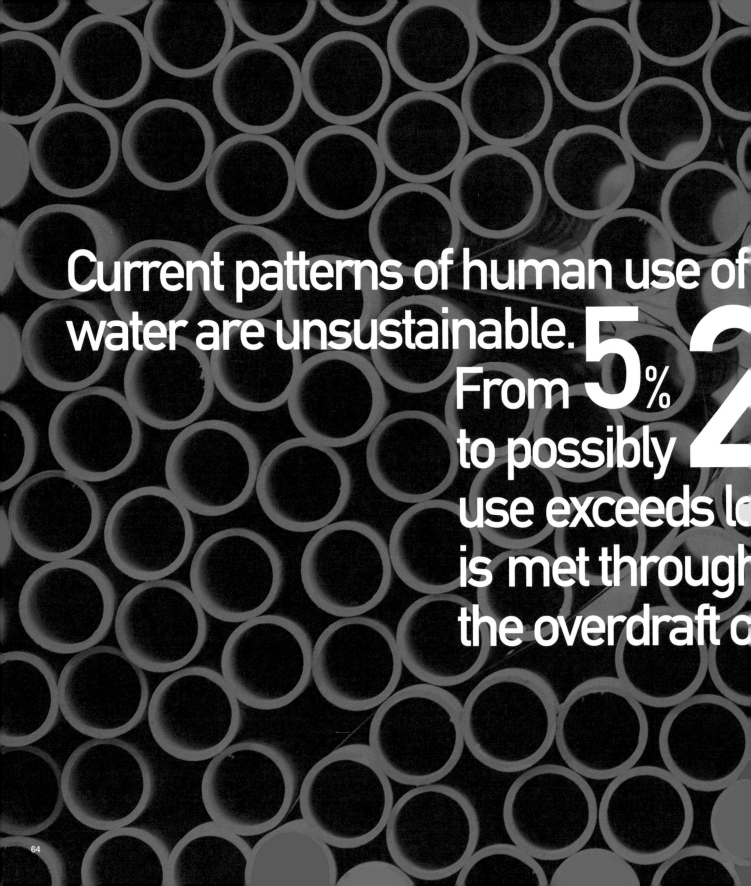

Current patterns of human use of water are unsustainable. From **5**% to possibly **2**... use exceeds l... is met through... the overdraft o...

5% of global freshwater term accessible supplies and ngineered water transfers or roundwater supplies. Millennium Ecosystem Assessment, 2005
Ecosystems and Human Wellbeing – Synthesis

BLUE ISSUE 01
OCTOBER 2009

LIVING SYSTEMS AT THE DEACERO HEADQUARTERS

Juan Porral
Associate Director

In collaboration with
Gabrielle Fladd, Rana Creek

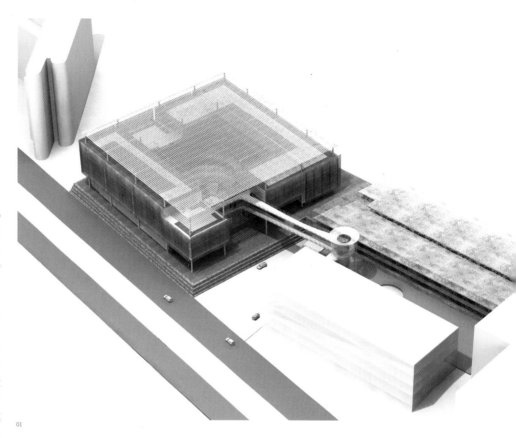

01

This article discusses how the design of the Deacero Headquarters evolved to include a strategy for using plants and landscape as a buildings' water filtration system, recycling grey and black water to become a net water producer.

Deacero is the second largest steel wire manufacturer in the world. It has its company headquarters in Monterrey, Mexico, with other facilities largely spread across the country and the USA. They are also a huge buyer of scrap steel throughout continental America. These scraps are freighted by train to their manufacturing plants where they are sorted and recycled, thus minimising the need for using more expensive virgin materials. Their experience running an efficient transportation and recycling programme resulted in company leadership being very receptive to environmentally responsible approaches, particularly those with decent payback periods.

Following significant growth throughout the previous decade, Deacero decided to build a new, larger headquarters building (DHQ). The selected site was adjacent to the existing HQ, and provided the flexibility to occupy both buildings as a corporate campus or to only occupy the new facility. Grimshaw was appointed towards the end of 2007 and from very early concept design the project was envisioned as providing the best and

healthiest possible workplace. Deacero also wanted a spacious indoor plaza to match the success of the existing outdoor plaza, located between the existing building and parking structure. These two priorities resulted in a narrow floor plate surrounding three sides of a central day-lit, four-storey atrium. The atrium is extensively planted and houses the main circulation to all departments. It also provides space for communal activities including a canteen, informal meeting areas, exhibition space, product library, reception, and even a small bank branch.

Another very important and resonating project goal emerged more gradually in the design process and encompassed a holistic approach to the valuable and scarce resource of water. Monterrey has very limited freshwater resources and with a combined sewer system flash flooding is a dangerous and common problem. On-site water re-use addresses these issues providing resource efficiency, reduced sewage loads, minimal infrastructure improvements and realisable financial return on investment. Project goals related to water included minimising potable water

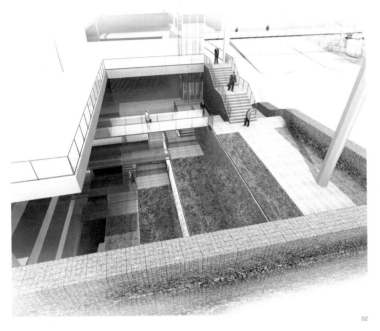

02   03

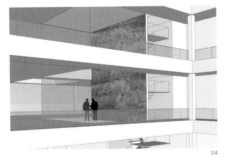

04

01   EARLY MASSING CONCEPT
02   LANDSCAPED TERRACES DOWN TO
     PARKING LEVELS BEFORE
     TRANSFORMATION INTO WETLANDS
03   EARLY STUDY OF CENTRAL ATRIUM
04   EARLY STUDY OF MULTI-STORY 'LIVING'
     WALL INSERTED INTO OFFICE FLOORPLATES

use for non-potable uses and a significant reduction in the volume of wastewater discharged into the municipal system. Deacero could not ignore the many benefits the realisation of these goals added to the project and so a water treatment and re-system became an integral component of the building design.

Local code dictates that municipal water is used to supply potable demand including sinks, lavatories, cleaning and pantries. This is roughly 29% of the building's total consumption. The remaining 71% of consumption is non-potable demand

for mechanical equipment, irrigation and toilets and can be supplied from on-site treated sources. In-depth analysis of building needs and water supply showed that treatment and reuse of all building wastewater including both gray and blackwater was to most economic and efficient strategy. Initially a system treating only graywater was considered, but this system was discarded because it required double plumbing throughout the building. This was a significant cost and resulted in the treatment and reuse of a small quantity of water compared to the current design. An integrated gray and blackwater treatment and reuse system uses a combination of biological and mechanical processes to treat 100% of building wastewater. The system manifests itself externally via significant water purification wetland terraces. This engineered wetland lines the entrance of the building from underground parking levels. Throughout the building water features and green walls complete the circuit and highlight the story of water.

Wastewater treatment is the biological, physical, and mechanical removal of water contaminants. Each of these treatment processes occurs at different stages within the system at DHQ. By using these processes in succession wastewater can be treated to a level considered safe by regulatory agencies for reuse. The essential functions of the wastewater treatment system are to reduce Biological Oxygen Demand (BOD), destroy pathogens, filter particulates, reduce nitrogen, phosphorous and Volatile Organic Compounds (VOCs) and stabilise or dispose of toxins. These treatment functions occur faster in constructed wetlands and biological systems than in conventional treatment systems.

Constructed wetlands are biologically complex systems, which adapt and respond to varying wastewater concentrations and changes in climate. The system is designed to emulate the systems that have naturally treated water in nature for millions of years. Naturally occurring wetlands encompass large areas and may treat water for an entire drainage basin. Studying how these

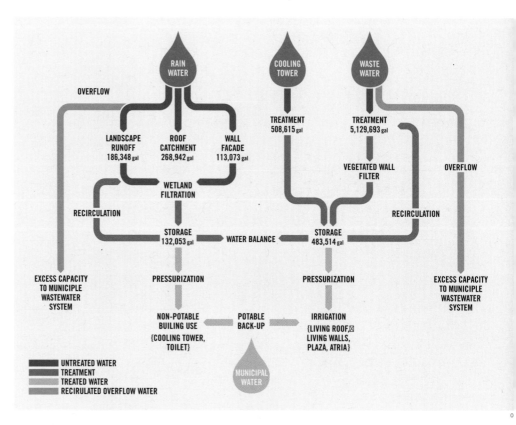

01 PROCESS FLOW DIAGRAM
THAT WAS INSTRUMENTAL
IN EXPLAINING TO THE
OWNER THE HOLISTIC
APPROACH TO WATER

systems function enables their re-creation for use in built environments. These urban wetlands are highly engineered, more efficient and able to function with less space than their natural counterparts.

The system at DHQ combines packaged biological treatment (a membrane bioreactor) with a constructed wetland to purify the water. All wastewater produced

in the building is collected and directed to the membrane bioreactor (MBR) where pathogens, VOCs, most toxins and large particles are removed. The MBR is sourced locally from one of the various companies that compete in this emerging market. Water is then disinfected with ultra-violet light. From there water is collected in a storage tank and pumped to the terraced

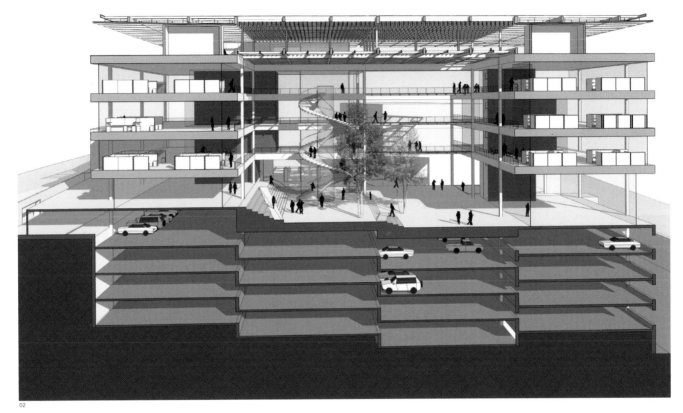

02

02 CROSS SECTION SHOWING
CENTRAL ATRIUM
SURROUNDED BY
OFFICES LOCATED ABOVE
UNDERGROUND PARKING

wetland in the parking garage. Since pathogens are removed by the MBR water can be free flowing across the surface of the wetland without any unpleasant sights or smells. The wetland provides 'polishing treatment.' After water emerges from the bioreactor it is 'lifeless' and still contains high nutrient levels. Plants and microbes in the wetland remove excess nutrients and breathe life back into the water improving the quality for irrigation use. The recirculation of the water from storage to wetlands and through the atrium water feature prevents bacteria from developing in the tank and the water from getting stagnant. After treatment in wetlands water is pumped back to storage and then re-circulated throughout the building for reuse in toilets, mechanical equipment and irrigation of all indoor and outdoor vegetated features.

One intriguing client request was that everyone, staff and visitors alike, enter the building in the same way. No special treatment was given to VIPs and no elevators go directly from parking to offices. The vast majority of staff arrive by car, and will

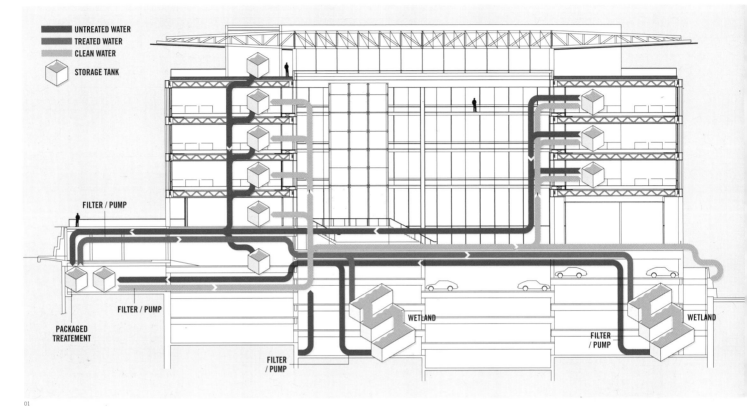

UNTREATED WATER
TREATED WATER
CLEAN WATER

STORAGE TANK

FILTER / PUMP

FILTER / PUMP

PACKAGED
TREATMENT

FILTER /
PUMP

WETLAND

FILTER
/ PUMP

WETLAND

01

01 DIAGRAM OF COMPLETE
    WETLAND SYSTEM
02 EARLY PROPOSAL FOR
    EXTENSIVE ROOF PLANTING
03 EARLY PROPOSAL FOR WATER
    TANKS BENEATH WETLANDS

continue to do so until Monterrey's public transportation improves. Therefore four levels of parking were required, three in the basement and one at-grade extending over most of the site. The entry 'Plaza' is directly above the parking facility and so designing a striking route up to the 'front door' at level two was a challenge. This main entry needed to be much more than simple staircases and became two large voids with a cascading set of terraces that comprises of interlaced stairs and planted areas. By providing two generous routes, each dealing with 50% of the garage capacity, the overall walking distance from parking was reduced.

These terraced planting areas quickly evolved into the treatment wetlands, integral to the gray and blackwater treatment system. The sound of water streaming down multiple waterfalls over four story's, together with smells from the fragrant planting and the colours of seasonal foliage and flowers feed the senses as one enters the building at the beginning of the day, or exits on the way home. Different textures in materials

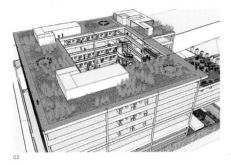

02

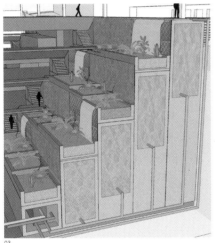

03

used to create the terracing can also be touched or viewed, completing the response to all of the senses. These wetlands are the only part of the water treatment system that is visible to staff and visitors alike. The wetlands manifest Deacero's stewardship of natural resources in a prominent way, enrich the experience of approaching and leaving and perform the more mundane task of masking the sounds from the parking garage and the busy adjacent highway.

Rana Creek, Landscape Architect and ecological consultant on the project, based the wetland design on the EPA Manual, '*Constructed Wetlands Treatment of Municipal Wastewaters*' and other sources such as:

- *Sizing of a Subsurface Flow Constructed Wetland for Onsite Domestic Wastewater Treatment*, an article from the document *On-site Wastewater Treatment*, M.C. Stecher, R.W. Weaver and K.J. McInnes
- *Hydraulic Conductivity of Onsite Constructed Wetlands* from the American Society of Agricultural and Biological Engineers

Studies were also done of preexisting systems to determine which strategies were most appropriate for implementation within the DHQ.

The client had concerns about potential smells from the treatment unit and the frequency and difficulty of system maintenance requirements. These concerns were overcome by visiting existing installations in Monterrey to talk with owners and maintenance staff. All were happy with the systems they were using and were very reassuring that maintenance was minimal and easy. A return on investment analysis showed net savings on up-front water costs and discharge fees of some US$35,000 per annum, which is about the capital cost of the blackwater treatment system. Therefore the system effectively pays for itself after one year. Continued annual savings will also cover wetland installation and system maintenance costs.

The volume of clean water saved from non-potable uses is significant, up to 14 million litres each year. That's 3 million litres more than the building's demand. It's amazing that in Mexico, a place with very scarce water resources, the system has resulted in the very unusual situation of having too much clean water. The design team is now working with Deacero to tap into the irrigation system of the adjacent, existing HQ to supply all of their irrigation demand as well. It is also a possibility that this extra water be donated to the city for use in irrigating the Av. Lazaro Cardenas streetscape. During dry months the city often does not have enough water to irrigate the streetscapes throughout Monterrey.

Both the short payback time of the wastewater treatment system and the increased water independency from municipal supplies contributed to selling the client on the water system. It was actually much harder to convince Deacero of the living roof, one of the main

01 **CENTRAL ATRIUM SEEN FROM THE THIRD FLOOR MAIN CIRCULATION ROUTE**
02 **FINAL IMAGE OF BUILDING SEEN FROM MAIN APPROACH**

01

features of the original design. This idea lost standing as the importance of the water system became clear. Eventually the living roof was value-engineered out of the project. However, it was later reinstated, due to its crucial role in stormwater mitigation, another goal of the project's holistic approach to water.

Stormwater is not collected for reuse at DHQ for various reasons. Weather patterns make collection difficult without an extremely large tank since Monterrey receives the majority of its rainfall all at one time while the rest of the year is very dry. Limited space in the building did not accommodate the required storage space. The wastewater treatment system was already supplying surplus water for reuse so incorporating stormwater into the

system was not justifiable. In arid climates, like that of Monterrey, localised wastewater treatment and reuse is the most efficient and economical reuse of water because the volume and frequency of the supply most closely matches the demand, minimising storage space requirements.

Instead of storage and reuse infiltration and filtration are the stormwater mitigation strategies employed. The building covers practically the entire site and the sub-grade is extremely compacted so infiltration into the ground was difficult. Instead, vegetated surfaces of the building retain and filter stormwater as it flows through the system. Rain falls on the multiple living roofs that perform primary biological treatment of the water. Stormwater flows over living walls and planted gabions

where additional treatment occurs. Then water is directed to infiltration planters in the landscape and finally overflows into the sewer. Maximising vegetated surfaces improves runoff quality and also reduces the rate of discharge. This strategy reasserts Deacero's position, as a responsible and attentive neighbour to the wider needs of the community.

Of course the living roofs and wetlands provide additional amenities for Deacero staff and visitors beyond their role in wastewater treatment and stormwater management. It is this holistic multiplicity of functionality of the Deacero 'green' features that provides additional value to the client and contributes to their primary objective of building the best possible workplace. ⊕

02

Globally, water quality is decli
industrial countries pathogen
surface waters has decrease
Nitrate concentration has gr
The capacity of ecosystems t
as evidenced by widespread
pollution. Loss of wetlands h
of ecosystems to filter and de

ng, although in most

d organic pollution of

over the last 20 years.

vn rapidly in the last 30 years.

urify such wastes is limited,

ports of inland waterway

further decreased the ability

mpose wastes.

Millennium Ecosystem Assessment, 2005
Ecosystems and Human Wellbeing – Synthesis

THE WATER THEATRE OF LAS PALMAS

Neven Sidor
Partner

01   THE NAMIBIAN FOG BEETLE
02   LAS PALMAS
03   PERSPECTIVE OF THE WATER
     THEATRE IN THE CONTEXT OF
     THE MASTERPLAN
04   CGI MODEL OF THE WATER
     THEATRE

Where the Atlantic Ocean meets Africa's Namib Desert, lives the Namibian Fog Beetle (Onymacris Unguicularis), endowed with an unusual evolutionary trait. Although this is an extremely dry part of the world, with as little as 5mm of rainfall per year, the prevailing sea breezes can be very humid, frequently giving rise to foggy conditions.

Our beetle's trick involves the geometry of its wings and its ability to regulate body temperature. It literally catches clouds. As an organism, all its hydration needs are met as it opens its wings to face the wind. When the temperature on their concave surface is below dew point fresh water droplets are formed. The beetle's body geometry then causes these droplets to run down to a small hollow where the fluid can be imbibed.

This article explains how such a small creature became the inspiration of an innovative, award-winning technology and then a proposal for an architectural icon at the heart of an island masterplan.

The town of Las Palmas grew along an isthmus at the northern tip of Gran Canaria, the largest of the Canary Islands. It was once a thriving tourist destination. However, in recent years the port on its eastern side has grown in size and significance to become a major ocean transhipment centre, and the town now lags only behind neighbouring Tenerife in tourist revenues.

The Grimshaw masterplan focused on coherence and enclosure. The majority of buildings specified in the brief were closely grouped together on just two sides of the new marina to create a backdrop completely screening the dockside cranes and containers beyond. The upper quay wall along the eastern edge of the isthmus was inhabited by bars and restaurants, interspersed with flights of external stairs leading to a large marine park immediately adjacent. This was laid out to reflect the distinctive circular depressions and walls traditionally used on the Canary Islands to shelter vines from sea winds as they grow in the volcanic soil. The marina edge was designed with the "Paseo" in mind, the traditional multi-generational Spanish habit of taking a gentle evening stroll around public places.

But where does the fog beetle come into it you may ask?

As we researched the local context, our attention was drawn to an acute mismatch between the island's population and the availability of natural spring water.

Despite its land mass and high extinct volcano, 77% of Gran Canaria's fresh water needs are currently met by a large reverse

FOR OUR PRACTICE, THE WATER THEATRE HAS BECOME EMBLEMATIC OF THE GREEN INFRASTRUCTURE REVOLUTION THAT URGENTLY NEEDS TO TAKE PLACE

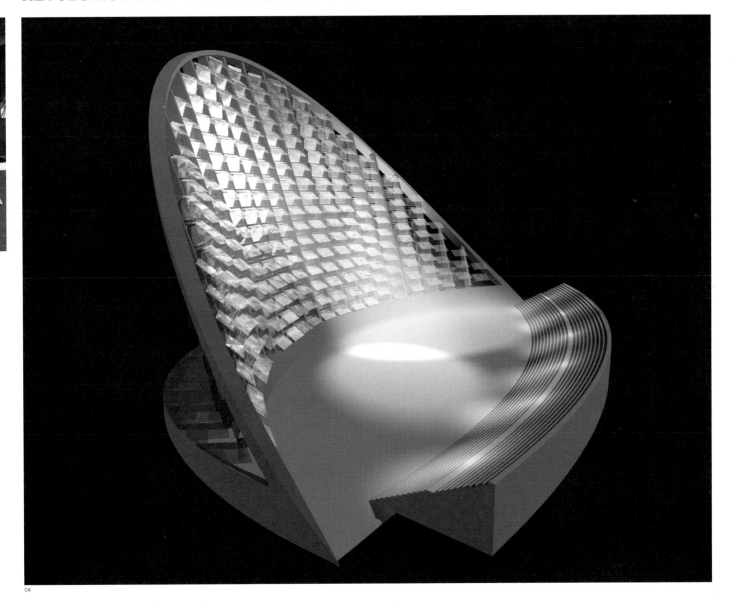

04

osmosis desalination plant. This makes the local economy very dependent on world oil prices. Moreover if the Mayor's aspirations to expand the tourist industry were to be successful, the island's population of 833,000 would be considerably enlarged. We therefore started to investigate more carbon neutral methods of desalination and came across the Seawater Greenhouse, an award-winning invention by the British industrial designer Charlie Paton. He had noticed the fog beetle's trick and developed it.

The Seawater Greenhouse is designed to grow vegetables in the desert without any power source other than the sun and moisture-laden sea breezes. A polytunnel is erected facing into the breeze. As air enters the structure its humidity is enhanced in an evaporator immediately before passing through a condenser. Fresh water simply drains off into a tray. It not only irrigates the earth troughs beyond, but also raises the transpiration level of the plants on account of the general increased humidity inside the main body of the solar heated enclosure. The reduced temperature of the condenser is achieved by pumping seawater through a web of plastic pipes, this being cooler than the desert shore during the day. After being warmed in the condenser salt water is pumped through a roof mounted solar collector before being used a second time in the evaporator as a warm spray over a honeycomb cardboard grid. The small pumps in the system are powered by photovoltaic cells.

01

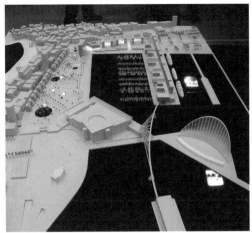

02

01 CGI IMAGE OF THE WATER
   THEATRE
02 MODEL OF THE LAS PALMAS
   MASTERPLAN WITH
   THE WATER THEATRE IN THE
   FOREGROUND

Charlie Paton agreed to join our competition team as a consultant. He quickly pointed out two striking facts about the Canary Islands. First, being volcanic, they are not surrounded by a continental shelf and depths of up to 1000 metres are unusually close to their beaches. It is therefore economic to pump seawater to land, having a relatively constant temperature of around 8 degrees centigrade. This is much cooler than the equivalent economically achievable seawater temperatures in Charlie's greenhouse. Second, the Canaries are subject to very constant trade winds, as can be seen not only from meteorological data, but also from the open crescent shape of the low rock walls sheltering the previously mentioned vineyards. Constant trade winds make it economic to build permanent structures facing them. Combine this with the availability of salt water at a constant temperature and you have the potential of desalination on a more industrial scale.

When we first approached Charlie we were thinking that his polytunnels could be incorporated into the roofscape of our harbour side buildings. However we were competing in a major international competition and were also acutely aware of the need for some kind of iconic gesture to assist with the marketing of this new quarter. Las Palmas would be vying with Tenerife and its new concert hall. Designed by Santiago Calatrava, the hall features a giant concrete wave emerging out of its roof. As an architectural practice we are uncomfortable with gratuitous shape making; we believe that to be truly satisfying an architectural form must be derived from multiple functions rather than from just a single one. The "Eureka Moment" came when the fog beetle, Charlie's invention, carbon free desalination, the Canary Island vineyard walls, the "Paseo" and the need for an architectural icon coalesced as a single idea. We call it the Water Theatre.

Imagine that you have just enjoyed some tapas by the marina. It is a pleasant warm evening (in Las Palmas it almost always is) and you have decided to join the local Spanish in their Paseo. You turn a corner and suddenly come across a large external amphitheatre. An acrobatic troupe is in the middle of their performance. Seating rakes down forming a crescent. However, behind the performers the space is completed by an extraordinary thing. An array of tilted glass louvres forming a concave upturned shell-like form with an elliptical outer edge rises up to a height of nearly 60 metres. The underside of the array is spectacularly floodlit and you notice a kinetic and iridescent quality. Inexplicably there is also the sound of a waterfall.

Intrigued you pick up a leaflet and discover that you have found the Water Theatre of Las Palmas, and that this is not just an open-air theatre by the water; it is a "theatre" where fresh water is created in front of your eyes. You read on and learn that the structure was aligned so that its convex outer edge faced into the prevailing winds and that each tilted glass louvre constitutes the visible part of a module of components,

not dissimilar to Charlie Paton's Seawater Greenhouse. There is a wall of honeycomb evaporators sprayed with warm seawater (the source of the waterfall sound). There is a wall of large diameter transparent flexible tubes with very cold seawater flowing through them. There are trays to collect the condensed fresh water, and there are tilted glass louvres with solar collectors on their upper surface and an iridescent coating on the underside. These are adjustable to control wind speed as air passes through the structure. Fresh water is piped off for distribution. Waste seawater is channelled off to irrigate marine plants in the new dockside park.

For now, the Water Theatre of Las Palmas remains just an idea. However

for our practice it has become emblematic of the green infrastructure revolution that urgently needs to take place. When Great Britain was first industrialised, power stations, viaducts, bridges, railway stations, dams and even sewage systems were seen as heroic ventures. They were often given pride of place within cities. Today they are seen as "undesirables", definitely not to be found in anyone's back yard. Our water theatre stands for the pressing need to recapture public imagination regarding green infrastructure projects so that they can inhabit our cities again, as indeed they must if society is going to address the environmental challenges it faces .....(and all on account of a small desert beetle). ⑧

01 **LONGITUDINAL SECTION**

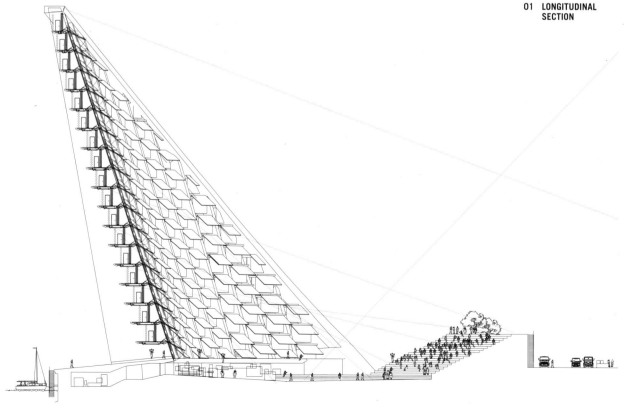

01

Over the past 50 years, ecosystems more rapidly in any comparable perio largely to meet rapidly g food, fresh water, timber resulted in a substantial loss in the diversity of lif

mans have changed
nd extensively than
f time in our history.
wing demands for
ibre, and fuel. This has
d largely irreversible
n Earth.

Millennium Ecosystem Assessment, 2005
Ecosystems and Human Wellbeing – Synthesis

EMBODIED ENERGY

Dominique Jenkins
Communications Manager

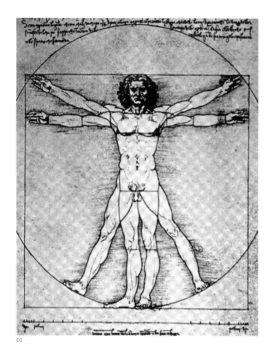

01

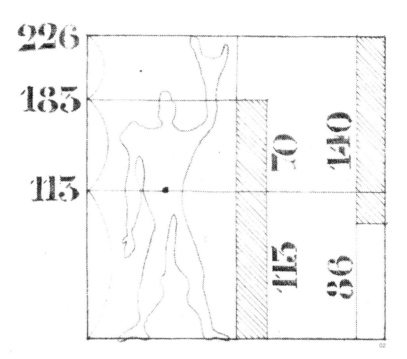

02

The London Festival of Architecture 2008 saw Grimshaw run a series of events exploring the theme Embodied Energy. These events, including talks, workshops, an exhibition and dance performances, catered to some 700 people and unfolded as an opportunity to explore architecture in a universally accessible way.

Embodied Energy started off with a simple question: how can we make architecture accessible to all?

From the outset the project team was keen to create a series of interactive, experiential events and to augment these with appropriate talks, workshops and an exhibition. The decision to use the human body, and dance specifically, to explore architecture came about for a number of reasons. Within an historical context, using the body to explore the built environment seemed natural; from Vitruvius to Le Corbusier the body has been key in determining architectural design, particularly with relation to proportion. More importantly, in a physiological context the human form was something everyone could identify with. Dance seemed the natural medium for this expression. It is essentially the choreography of space and, as such, can be understood as the organic and experiential counterpart to architecture's more structured and corporeal choreography of space.

Early research led the team to look closely at the Bauhaus and Oskar Schlemmer's Space Dance in particular. Investigations into the relationship between dance and architecture – notation systems and ways of understanding, tracking and mapping space – were all examined.

Energy and understanding its consumption became central to the project. An early idea was to grow raw materials in

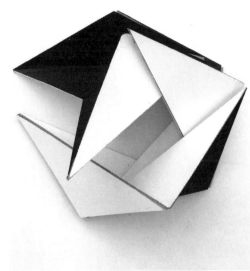

01 DA VINCI'S VITRUVIAN MAN
02 MODULOR BY LE CORBUSIER
03 OSKAR SCHLEMMER'S
   TRIADIC BALLET
04 COSTUME MODEL
05 REHEARSAL WITH COSTUME
   PROTOTYPE

the office and then weave these to create some sort of structure/s which the dancers could manipulate.

After experiments with willow, bamboo and pampas grass, it emerged that growth in-house would be impossible. Outsourcing was also quickly discounted once it was realised that suppliers sourced their plants overseas. However the basic idea to use dance and structures to explore architecture had struck a chord with the team and a choreographer and dancers were appointed.

Contemporary dance was best suited to the team's aims and through established dance centre The Place, Katie Green, a young choreographer was brought on board. One of her previous works – a study of bodies manipulating boxes and creating moving structures – seemed to align at an elemental level with the team's vision. Six dancers from the London Contemporary Dance School at The Place were also selected and weekly workshop sessions began.

Very early on the structures came to be referred to as costumes; the team felt the objects should be more intimately connected with the dancers than the word "structures" suggested. These costumes emerged over a period of six months. Initially the team explored a series of different mediums including smooth sheet and ribbon-like surfaces, peacock forms and hooped objects. Eventually a series of origami-like structures that could be linked together to create larger forms were developed.

The costumes were made up of four modular facets that joined to create a series of different sized hinged chevrons. Materials such as vinyl, latex, aluminium honeycomb and glass were all investigated, but the final product was constructed from a recycled paper honeycomb panel. Manufactured in the UK by Dufaylite, these costumes can be broken down and recycled. The hinges were formed from thermoplastic profile extrusions manufactured using recycled PVC and can either be reused or chopped down and recycled.

The choreography for the piece was developed simultaneously with the costumes; as the costumes changed and

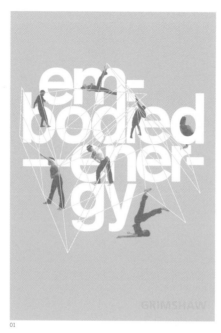
01

evolved, so did the choreography. Research at performance sites generated very different responses; the Royal Academy (RA) courtyard, where the dance piece would premiere, was driven by its very formal environment and the Anthony Caro sculptures temporarily on display there. Outside of the RA, the sites were much less formal, and as a consequence the choreography could be less structured and more responsive to the sites and the audiences they attracted. The intention was to try and establish a very direct relationship with the audiences, engaging and involving them

02

03

01   PROMOTIONAL GRAPHICS
02   DANCE REHEARSAL IN THE
        ROYAL ACADEMY COURTYARD
03   THE DANCE TROUPE AT THE
        RA IN FRONT OF SCULPTURES
        BY ANTHONY CARO

to make their experience as interactive as possible. The choreography attempted to do this by blurring the lines between "stage" and "non-stage": dancers passed in and around observers and those walking past or through the sites.

Responses and audiences at the various sites differed dramatically; the RA performances generally attracted dance professionals, architects and designers, whereas the other locations were often chanced upon by locals or passers-by. Feedback from all was encouraging, with one journalist describing the RA piece as follows:

"The dancers moved in predetermined paths, translated through choreography into spatial movement resulting in [an] intimate integration of design and dance. There was an element of abstraction ... as structure became part of the dancer's kinesphere, interlocking man-made with the organic in movement, producing a geometrical fluidity and experience of space through structure."

Embodied Energy allowed us a unique opportunity to work across disciplines on a constantly evolving and ultimately ethereal project. The multi-disciplinary approach provided opportunities to explore new thinking and allowed us to refocus our architectural efforts on the individual. Attendance at, and interest in, these events suggests that we were successful in our original aim of making architecture accessible to all. This was reinforced by the high level of enthusiastic contribution we experienced. The project continues to resonate influencing the way we design spaces and reinforcing the idea that buildings are defined by the choreography of these spaces and the way individuals use them. **ⓑ**

Our global footprint is now above

te

30% of the planets biological capacity support life on earth

World Wilderness Foundation
Living Planet Report 2006

LONDON FESTIVAL OF ARCHITECTURE:
IN CONVERSATION

01

02

In July 2008, Grimshaw opened its doors to the public for a week-long series of events entitled Embodied Energy. These events, part of the London Festival of Architecture 2008, climaxed in an evening of talks and debates on the 15th July 2008.

The keynote debate focused on the environment and architecture and was chaired by Jon Snow, an award-winning journalist who has anchored Channel 4 News since 1989. The speakers were John Vidal, Environmental Editor for the Guardian, Tim Smit, Founder of the Eden Project and the Lost Gardens of Heligan and Professor Michael Braungart, chemist and acclaimed co-author of Cradle to Cradle: Remaking the Way We Make Things.

The debate brought together several themes explored throughout the week's events. At its heart was the question 'What role do architects play in a sustainable future?' but the conversation also explored issues such as material use, resourcing, the politics of sustainability and personal motivations.

Here, we reproduce an edited transcript of the conversation, highlighting the key issues.

01 THE AUDIENCE GATHER IN THE ATRIUM OF GRIMSHAW'S LONDON OFFICE
02 JON SNOW
03 THE KEYNOTE DEBATE
04 MICHAEL BRAUNGART

03

Jon Snow: *We're talking about sustainability, the future, whether architecture can play any role whatsoever in a sustainable future. I am really amazed at what measures people are taking to try and create sustainable buildings and offerings. That's not to say that all of these have been taken up, but the ideas seem to be there. Michael, why don't you start us off, is the Cradle to Cradle concept leaving political leadership out in the cold or are they party to it?*

Michael Braungart: The interesting thing in the US is that President Bush was somehow very beneficial because he made it clear the government doesn't do anything, which is better than with someone like Al Gore. Gore's film shows he knew about the greenhouse effect. He was vice-president of the United States for eight years, didn't do anything (about climate change) and then he wins a Nobel prize for it. So the point is, if you think 'I could really do something' then don't wait for the government.

JS: *John, it is possible to have change without political revolution?*

John Vidal: I've just come back from Malawi, where we have a little project. We gave them £400 and they built themselves a library and it's the most sustainable architecture I've ever seen.

Somewhere like Malawi is Cradle to Cradle anyway. People want to do something and they will do it. You don't need a degree in architecture, you just have to know what is most suitable for your own aims. Problem is, here in Britain we can't get our head around the word sustainable and actually it's quite simple.

JS: *And of course, the truth is we look to political leadership for environmental change. Tim, did you build Eden in spite of, because of, or together with political leadership?*

Tim Smit: Political leadership sounds like an oxymoron to me. I think, everyone is now so tuned to a narrative that makes people feel they can be part of something bigger than themselves. I'm really optimistic because I think for all the doom and gloom in our culture, of society going down the pan, you only have to scratch the surface and we find people yearning to be more than the sum of their parts.

04

'PRESIDENT BUSH WAS SOMEHOW VERY BENEFICIAL BECAUSE HE MADE IT CLEAR THE GOVERNMENT DOESN'T DO ANYTHING'

Michael Braungart

01

'WE'LL PROBABLY LOOK BACK ON THIS PERIOD AS A BLESSED ONE IN A BIZARRE WAY, WE'RE KIND OF TWENTY YEARS AHEAD OF WHERE WE'RE SUPPOSED TO BE'

John Vidal

JV: We'll probably look back on this period as a blessed one in a bizarre way, we're kind of twenty years ahead of where we're supposed to be. We thought the price of oil would rise to $150 per barrel, in 2030, but actually it's right now and this is a phenomenal change and we have to confront how we live, how we feed ourselves. None of us have given this any real thought, we've all insulated ourselves to say, well that is the future, will the earth be able to cope, but it's happening right now. And that's fantastically exciting and it's what we desperately need to get us out of the oil age. As architects, commentators and facilitators we're in an immensely privileged position to actually see it happen right under our eyes, so the revolution is here, fantastic, great.

JS: *Michael, where does the price of oil fit into the Cradle to Cradle formula?*

MB: The material part is more critical than the energy side. So it's amazing that people always talk about the stupid energy side, because the material side is so much more critical. With solar power, we will learn to harness the sun, so whenever oil prices rise, that's no problem, because we have the sun. But copper is so much rarer than oil and the copper recycling rate was never so low as today. So it's nice to talk about energy and oil, but the survival path of materials is so much more critical and nobody has any awareness.

02

03

'WE'VE ALWAYS TALKED ABOUT DEMOCRACY AS BEING BASED ON A VOTE BUT WE DON'T GIVE PEOPLE ENOUGH INFORMATION TO MAKE GOOD DECISIONS'

Tim Smit

1 JOHN VIDAL
2 AUDIENCE MEMBERS INCLUDING SIR NICHOLAS GRIMSHAW, FAR LEFT AND NEVEN SIDOR, THIRD FROM RIGHT
3 TIM SMIT

Neven Sidor (Audience): *Do we see democracy as a positive thing or a means by which the electorate can delude itself and blame politicians for what is actually their fault?*

JS: *My answer would be that I think people are waiting to be told what to do and nobody wants to tell them. What do you think Tim?*

TS: I totally agree with that. I think the trouble in Britain is we've always talked about democracy as being based on a vote but we don't give people enough information to make good decisions. In Cornwall right now we're actively discussing this. There is quite a spirit of independence going on. People are saying 'Crikey, if we wait much longer, we're at the end of the power lines, the end of the gas lines, everyone else will be fucked and we'll be the first ones as everyone will cut us off'. It's amazing how over the last year this has gone from science fiction to real hair on the back of the neck stuff.

JV: You know, we couldn't have had this conversation five years ago. We've moved so far, so fast that we're really pushing ourselves in terms of science and ecology, coming to terms with the earth in a very different way. It's the biggest change we've ever seen. Our children will not recognise the way we built buildings or how we live. It will seem positively archaic. Let's get used to rethinking ourselves and revolutionise how we live, how we work, play, communicate.

JV: I think we have really mucked it up – big time and if we can start rethinking how we live and mimicking nature, we're going to go a long way. But we have to start by tuning ourselves first.

MB: We need to look at other species and start to be good, rather than less bad. We see buildings like trees, but look at a tree, it makes oxygen and water, a tree supports climate, it is beneficial. What we see now is mostly bad architecture and that's not enough. We need to start to make beneficial architecture.

TS: We have only 2 days worth of food for this nation in supermarkets and we live with complete amnesia of the effects of this. Jolyon Brewis and I were saying the real cool architects are going to start looking at buildings not just as icons but as fields of dreams that will actually be able to grow plants. With a great planning regime, you could grow almost as many crops on a building as would be needed to feed the people inside them.

JS: *No-one has yet risen to that challenge, for an architect to build a house that will generate enough food to feed the people within it. Can it be done?*

TS: Yeah it can be done. What should architects be looking at for the future? I think we've got it wrong all the time and I think bringing the social into the consideration is fantastic.

The future might not be about ownership, but about reinventing Unitarianism. I think this is a really encouraging way for us to be looking at our future, these social realignments could be really very positive. So when people say we're doomed, I think no actually we're not fucking doomed. It's cynicism that kills us – if you dare to believe that you can get 100's and 1000's of people working together to do wonderful things, you'll have a hell of a lot more fun. I think it's such an exciting time to be alive.

MB: I am more specifically into materials, I'm working with two dozen architects as their, as Madonna would say, material boy, so I'm choosing to make materials for them to go back into cycles e.g. we make concrete that absorbs toxins, which actually cleans air. It's not only vegetation, it is building material which can help us change completely.

JV: Architects are going to be responsible for buildings that are going to let us all down or get us all going. But, you don't have an ethic as far as I can see, you don't have an oath like doctors, so why don't you? You should get together and say we'll have an architectural ethic. At some point, if you guys believe in the science, you will have to play your part, that's your responsibility. ⓑ

01

02

01 JON SNOW
02 AUDIENCE MEMBERS
03 JON SNOW CHATS WITH
    SIR NICHOLAS GRIMSHAW
04 JON SNOW, TIM SMIT
    AND JOLYON BREWIS

03

04

GRIMSHAW

57 Clerkenwell Road
London
EC1M 5NG
UK

T +44 (0)20 7291 4141
F +44 (0)20 7291 4194

100 Reade Street
New York
NY 10013
USA

T +1 212 791 2501
F +1 212 791 2173

494 LaTrobe Street
Melbourne
VIC 3000
Australia

T +61 (0) 3 9321 2600
F +61(0) 3 9321 2611

info@grimshaw-architects.com
www.grimshaw-architects.com